"Faith is a passion, and the only men who understand it are those who understand it passionately."

p. 131

PASSION, "KNOWING HOW," AND UNDERSTANDING

AMERICAN ACADEMY OF RELIGION

DISSERTATION SERIES

edited by

H. Ganse Little, Jr.

Number 9

PASSION, "KNOWING HOW," AND UNDERSTANDING

An Essay on the Concept of Faith

by

Andrew J. Burgess

SCHOLARS PRESS
Missoula, Montana

PASSION, "KNOWING HOW," AND UNDERSTANDING

An Essay on the Concept of Faith

by

Andrew J. Burgess

Published by

SCHOLARS PRESS

for

The American Academy of Religion

Distributed by

SCHOLARS PRESS
University of Montana
Missoula, Montana 59801

PASSION, "KNOWING HOW," AND UNDERSTANDING

An Essay on the Concept of Faith

by

Andrew J. Burgess
Case Western Reserve University
Cleveland, OH 44106

Ph.D., 1969　　　　　　　　　　　　　　　　　　Advisor:
Yale University　　　　　　　　　　　　　　　Paul L. Holmer

Copyright © 1975

by

The American Academy of Religion

Library of Congress Cataloging in Publication Data

Burgess, Andrew J
　　Passion, "knowing how," and understanding.

　　(Dissertation series--American Academy of Religion ; no. 9)
　　Originally presented as the author's thesis, Yale, 1969: under the title: The concept of passionate faith, Kierkegaard and analytical philosophy of mind.
　　Bibliography: p.
　　1. Faith.　2. Emotions.　3. Kierkegaard, Søren Aabye, 1813-1855.　4. Analysis (Philosophy)　I. Title. II. Series: American Academy of Religion. Dissertation series - American Academy of Religion ; no. 9.
BV4637.B88　1975　　　121'.7　　　75-31550
ISBN 0-89130-044-9

Printed in the United States of America
1 2 3 4 5
Printing Department
University of Montana
Missoula, Montana 59801

TABLE OF CONTENTS

	Page
PREFACE	vii
INTRODUCTION	ix
ABBREVIATIONS	xvii

CHAPTER ONE   THE CONFLICT BETWEEN PASSION AND REASON . . 1

- A. Descartes and the Mechanism of the Passions . . . 1
- B. The "Traditional View" on the Passions 5
    1. The Regularity Theory 5
    2. The Rationalistic Theory 8
- C. Ordinary Language Theories 13
    1. Ryle: Emotions as Dispositions 14
    2. Bedford: Emotions as Appraisals 21
    3. Peters: Emotions as Distortions 24
- D. The Conflict of Passion and Reason 31
- E. Conclusions 36

CHAPTER TWO   CLIMACUS: "FAITH IS A HAPPY PASSION" . . . 39

- A. Theses Attributable to Johannes Climacus 39
- B. The "How" and the "What" 43
- C. The Mutual Fit of the "How" and the "What" . . . 47
    1. If Subjectivity is Truth 48
    2. If Subjectivity is Untruth 52
- D. Faith and the Conflict of Passion and Reason . . . 58
    1. The Regularity Theory: Ryle 58
    2. The Rationalistic Theory: Spinoza and Peters . 59
    3. The Analogy Between Faith and Love 62
- E. Passion, Knowledge, and Faith 63

CHAPTER THREE   "KNOWING HOW" AND RELIGIOUS BELIEF . . . 65

- A. "Knowing How" and "Knowing That" 65
    1. Ryle and "Knowing How" 65
    2. Analyzing "Knowing That" as "Knowing How" . . 68
    3. Martin: Kinds of "Knowing How" 70
    4. The Category of "Knowing How" 75
- B. Problems in Using "Knowing How" as a Category in Religion 76
    1. Schmidt 76
    2. Braithwaite 80
    3. Nielsen 83
    4. Variations in the Dispositional Analysis of Religious Belief 88
    5. Conclusion 89

Contents

Page

CHAPTER FOUR   FAITH AND UNDERSTANDING: A CONTEMPORARY
DEBATE   93

A. The "Linguistic Pluralists" and Religious Belief .   94
B. The "Linguistic Monists" and Religious Belief . .   98
    1. MacIntyre   99
    2. MacIntyre vs. Evans-Pritchard and Winch . . .   101
    3. The Case for Linguistic Monism   106
C. Third Phase: The Response of the "Pluralists" . .   108
    1. Winch's Response to MacIntyre   108
    2. Systematically Ambiguous Concepts   110
    3. Problems in the Pluralistic Position   111
    4. Passionate Disagreement   113
D. Conclusions and Correctives   116
    1. The End of a Debate   116
    2. Essentially Contested Concepts   117
    3. The Concept of Passionate Faith   121

CHAPTER FIVE   CONCLUSION   125

A. Dispositional Analysis   125
B. Kierkegaard and Wittgenstein   129

BIBLIOGRAPHY   133

PREFACE

At the suggestion of several readers the original title of this dissertation, "The Concept of Passionate Faith: Kierkegaard and Analytical Philosophy of Mind," has been changed, in order to indicate better the breadth of the essay.

Despite the change in title, however, Kierkegaard's role in the argument ought not to be overlooked. Although no attempt has been made to represent his views fully, even on the topics discussed, the theses selected serve an important function, in that they test the adequacy of various theories about passion, "knowing how," and understanding as they apply to faith. The richness of his descriptions of the Christian faith sets an exacting standard against which oversimplifications may be measured. Without this Kierkegaardian backdrop for the argument I would never have dared embark upon the essay at all. It would have been too easy, and too misleading, to rely simply on one's own hunches about the nature of faith. I believe that exact and fruitful discussion of faith cannot come about in contemporary philosophy unless the discussants take seriously the classic statements about faith, and unless historical scholars, for their part, accept what I call in the Introduction their "extramural" task.

This essay could not have been written without the help of many people. I am particularly grateful to Professor Howard Hong, who introduced me to the study of Kierkegaard and to "Johannes Climacus," and who also kindly allowed me to use materials from the unpublished volumes of his translation of Kierkegaard's journals and papers.

In the preparation of the text indispensable assistance was given by a number of people, among whom I am especially indebted to Professors William Christian and Donald Saliers.

I am also very thankful to Professor Hans Frei, who encouraged and guided me in the publication of this dissertation, and to Professor Gerald McCulloh, the editor of the former Nineteenth Century Theology dissertation series, for which the work was originally nominated.

Preface

    Finally, I wish to express my gratitude to my advisor, Professor Paul Holmer, who provided me with inspiration and constant aid. The blame for the shortcomings which remain is, of course, mine alone; they would have been greater but for Professor Holmer's interest and help.

INTRODUCTION

The purpose of this extended essay is to discuss problems concerning the relationships, within the context of the Christian faith, among concepts of knowing, believing, and feeling. The locus for these problems is the general question: How far and in what ways is the sharing of a distinctive mode of passions a prerequisite for learning the Christian truth? In what sense, if at all, must one say that the possession of certain emotions--joy, love, and peace, for example--is internally or conceptually related to the holding of Christian convictions about God, the world, or anything else? The question applies not simply to the *holding* of these convictions (for someone might easily grant that convictions have some sort of emotional concomitant) but even to the serious *entertaining* of the possibility of adopting these convictions, at least in the sense that entertaining them seriously means to grasp the "point" of believing that way even if one does not choose to share the belief.

A. Methodological Restrictions

Taken in a comprehensive way the question just cited defies adequate treatment, since it involves a host of very general issues concerning the relative places of dispassionate inquiry and personal commitment. Accordingly, this essay restricts itself methodologically in two ways:

(1) by raising the issues within a particular philosophical tradition, principally that of "analytic philosophy," and

(2) by drawing upon a part of the writings of a certain philosopher of religion, Søren Kierkegaard.

Both aspects of the inquiry call for some comment:

1. The Use of Analytic Philosophy

Along with the rest of modern thought, analytic philosophy inherits the legacy of Descartes. The warfare between passion and reason, an opposition implicit in the Cartesian argument, arises again in various ways within twentieth century writings, most obviously (and also most crudely) in positivism's "Great Divide" between the cognitive and the emotive. But there are differences between the old and new ways of putting the question which should not be overlooked. The contemporary methodology which urges upon philosophers the need to pay attention to everyday examples and to distinctions embedded in ordinary language provides tools for investigating subtleties and ambiguities in conceptual relationships which the earlier thinkers did not possess. There is, it is true, a persistent and rather disheartening tendency among some analytic philosophers of religion to fall back on the worn-out categories of faculty psychology by means of the terms "cognitive," "conative," and "emotive." Yet this result need not discourage us from using the approach of analytic philosophy in large part. For it may be that the difficulty arises not from following an inadequate methodology, but from not following the method far enough.

2. The Use of Kierkegaard

As a guide to the nature of Christian discourse Kierkegaard has a special place within this essay. This is not the first time he has been chosen for such a role by those working within the analytic tradition,[1] nor is it likely to be the last. Although Kierkegaard's pages are often dense and difficult, they repay the effort they require. Kierkegaard's intense honesty, which keeps him from accepting oversimplified solutions to difficulties in the Christian faith, together with his sensitivity to distinctions among the functions of different kinds of discourse and his appreciation for the value of concrete examples--all make him an invaluable mentor in the philosophy of religion.

There are, nevertheless, obstacles in the way of anyone who tries to employ Kierkegaard within a systematic inquiry. Chief among these is the problem of pseudonymity. Kierkegaard's procedure of ascribing many of his writings (mostly those which he called his "Literature") to pseudonyms is one of the puzzling aspects of his work. Not that anyone is uncertain who it was who penned the words. The presence of the names of Nicholas

---

[1] E.g., J. Heywood Thomas, *Subjectivity and Paradox* (Oxford, 1957), and the writings by Winch, Phillips, and Malcolm which are cited in Chapter Four, *infra*, esp. pp. 97, 114.

Introduction

Notabene, Hilarius Bookbinder, Johannes the Seducer, or any of the others on a title page was not expected to deceive anyone in Kierkegaard's day and will not do so now. But because Kierkegaard exercised care in matching each imaginary author to the appropriate opinion and arranged these authors according to an overall strategy in his authorship, it is frequently of the utmost importance to ascertain the reason for the use of a particular pseudonym. Consequently scholars who are trying to investigate these books find themselves involved in discussions--and frequently very prolonged and heated ones at that--over the title pages, before they ever get to the text itself.

The approach here will be to circumvent the problem of pseudonymity by picking one of the pseudonymous authors, Johannes Climacus, and discussing his views as if he had been an existing, independent thinker.[2] The reader will quickly accustom himself to treating Climacus as a real person, and in order to prevent anyone from becoming historically confused about who did in fact write the *Fragments* and the *Postscript* there are also a number of allusions in the text to "Kierkegaard's Climacus writings." For the reader's slight trouble in this matter he will be rewarded by being spared lengthy treatment of the pseudonymity question. It is, of course, still very pertinent to ask how the views of Climacus represented here relate to Kierkegaard's authorship as a whole, but beyond a few necessary references and comparisons that topic will not be dealt with in the present essay.

The propriety of fastening upon one pseudonym, and upon Johannes Climacus in particular, exists because:

(1) Kierkegaard took great pains to delineate each pseudonymous author as an independent author in style and

---

[2]Other recent studies which have limited themselves in this way include: Herbert M. Garelick, *The Anti-Christianity of Kierkegaard: A Study of the* Concluding Unscientific Postscript (The Hague, 1965); Garelick, "The Irrationality and Suprarationality of Kierkegaard's Paradox," *Southern Journal of Philosophy*, II (Summer, 1964), pp. 75-86; and Henry E. Allison, "Christianity and Nonsense," *Review of Metaphysics*, XX (March, 1967), pp. 432-60.

Introduction

viewpoint,[3] and in the case of Climacus even supplied us with considerable "biographical" information and with a writing which purports to come from Climacus' youth.[4]

(2) Climacus' standpoint comes close in many respects to Kierkegaard's own views.[5]

(3) Even in his private papers Kierkegaard frequently refers to these writings as the opinions of Johannes Climacus.[6]

(4) The *Philosophical Fragments* and the *Concluding Unscientific Postscript*, the writings ascribed to Climacus (along

---

[3] That each of the pseudonyms in Kierkegaard's authorship is distinctive in both style and content has long been recognized. The fact has been recently supported by a study carried on with computer techniques by Alastair McKinnon entitled "Kierkegaard's Pseudonyms: A New Hierarchy," *American Philosophical Quarterly*, VI (April, 1969), pp. 116-26.

[4] The volume has been published as *Johannes Climacus or, De Omnibus Dubitandum Est*, trans. Croxall (Stanford, 1958).

[5] Niels Thulstrup, asking whether the *Fragments* is "genuinely pseudonymous" in the sense that it "has content which Kierkegaard would not vouch for, would not adhere to," puts the matter this way: "The answer to this question must be: the work is both thought and written in Kierkegaard's own name and therefore cannot be considered a truly pseudonymous work. If one compares the thought both with the entries in Kierkegaard's *Journals* of the same period, the first half of the year 1844, and with the *Edifying Discourses* from the same time, extensions and sharpening of thought can certainly be found, and one can also find much that is new in *Philosophical Fragments*; but one will find hardly any inconsistency between this work and the other private and published thought and writing. *Philosophical Fragments* undoubtedly represents Kierkegaard's own view at the time it was written and published. To say this, however, is not to affirm that the work provides a full picture of Kierkegaard's views." Commentator's Introduction to *Philosophical Fragments*, trans. Hong (Princeton, 1962), p. lxxxv.

The *Fragments* truly if incompletely presents Kierkegaard's views of 1844, so far as the literary form he chose allows him. Kierkegaard's massive commentary on the *Fragments*, called the *Postscript*, avows on the other hand to be by Johannes Climacus who "does not give himself out to be a Christian," but is a "humorist" (one in the transition between Religiousness A and Religiousness B) (p. 545); and this is surely not Kierkegaard's own stance at the time, though it is closer to the Christian viewpoint than the other writings in the "Literature." In addition to their intrinsic interest, then, these two works are important as indications of Kierkegaard's position.

[6] See, e.g., *infra*, page 41, footnote 7, referring to X^2 A 299.

Introduction

with the unpublished *De Omnibus Dubitandum Est*, the youthful effort), are the works most commonly singled out by philosophers to represent Kierkegaard's opinions.

B. Nature and Outline of the Essay

1. Nature of the Presentation

The purpose of the essay is not primarily to provide an exposition of analytic philosophy or of Kierkegaard's views, but by developing certain parallel themes in contemporary analytic philosophy of mind and in Kierkegaardian scholarship to open the way for the application of insights from both sources to certain systematic puzzles in the philosophy of religion.

Within the arena of Kierkegaardian research, accordingly, this essay occupies a distinctly minority position. The effort of scholars of Kierkegaard during the past decades has been largely absorbed with topics of historical interest. Besides the biographical studies of Kierkegaard many competent analyses of his thought as a whole have been published, and the stream shows no sign of diminishing, as new materials are discovered and as new perspectives open up which force a re-evaluation of his writings. Accompanying these is a helpful group of monographs which traces historical roots of his work or structural similarities of his thought to that of other men--"Kierkegaard and" investigations. Here again no end of the production is in sight. Recently, moreover, there has been an increasing number of studies of an aspect or motif of his thought, such as irony, discipleship, or suffering.

All such approaches to Kierkegaardian scholarship are in a sense intramural: they are carried on within the precincts of a restricted body of source materials and historical relationships. The special character of Kierkegaard's authorship with its multiplicity of viewpoints demands that, more than most figures in the history of philosophy and of Christianity, he be accorded this sort of constant scholarly escort.

Kierkegaard's extramural relationships to the contemporary scene have received much less attention. In a typical volume of Kierkegaardiana they turn up in the last chapter, after the questions of biography, historical antecedents, the "stages," indirect method, and the like have exhausted the energy of the writer. One is reminded of Kierkegaard's comparison of a professor's prolegomenon to a man trying to make a broad jump. The broad jumper decides to give himself the longest possible running start and begins a full mile back--but by the time he reaches the take-off point he is so tired that he cannot jump at all!

It is to this second or "extramural" task, the investigation of Kierkegaard's contribution to the current philosophical and theological scene, that the present essay is dedicated. In assuming this assignment the essay takes over for its own purposes the results of much historical investigation. Perhaps in the course of the very different investigations undertaken here some light will also be shed on matters of the exposition of Kierkegaard's text. For new philosophical tools will be suggested which may reveal more clearly Kierkegaard's enduring bequest to theology and philosophy, over and beyond his criticism of the nineteenth century Idealistic milieu. And when new questions are put to Kierkegaard in this way, or old questions with a fresh slant, it will be surprising if the understanding of the text remains just the same as before. In any case, the way is open for others to refine the Kierkegaard interpretation in the following pages. Such criticism is not only invited, it is demanded, by the kind of project represented here.

2. Outline of the Argument

The discussion in the following chapters centers on the statement by Kierkegaard's Climacus "Faith is a happy passion."

The first chapter takes up the familiar doctrine of a warfare between passion and reason, and discusses the effects which this teaching has had in the treatment of the concept of passion. The traditional understanding of the passions by Descartes, Spinoza, and Hume is contrasted with the contemporary dispositional analyses.

The second chapter introduces the context in the *Fragments* and the *Postscript* of the saying "Faith is a happy passion," by way of the distinctions both between the "how" and the "what," and between "Subjectivity is truth" and "Subjectivity is untruth."

Introduction

The third chapter reviews the dispositional analysis of the concept of knowledge which is given in the "knowing how"/"knowing that" distinction, and then goes on to compare some contemporary dispositional treatments of the problems of faith and knowledge with the position of Kierkegaard's Climacus.

The fourth chapter brings the Climacean definition of faith into a current debate in the philosophy of religion over the possibility of communication between believers and skeptics. The implications of the statements that "Subjectivity is truth" and "Subjectivity is untruth" and the notions of the "happy passion" (faith) and the "unhappy passion" (offense) are explored to discover their relevance to the question of the relationship between faith and understanding.

ABBREVIATIONS

Periodicals

APQ	*American Philosophical Quarterly*
JP	*Journal of Philosophy*
PAS	*Proceedings of the Aristotelian Society*
PASS	*Proceedings of the Aristotelian Society, Supplementary Volume*
PQ	*Philosophical Quarterly*
PR	*Philosophical Review*
Rel. Stud.	*Religious Studies*
Rev. Met.	*Review of Metaphysics*

Kierkegaard Materials

Fragments   Johannes Climacus, pseud. *Philosophical Fragments or A Fragment of Philosophy*. Translated by David F. Swenson and Howard V. Hong. Princeton, N. J.: Princeton University Press, 1962.

De Omnibus   Johannes Climacus, pseud. *Johannes Climacus or, De Omnibus Dubitandum Est and a Sermon*. Translated by T. H. Croxall. Stanford, California: Stanford University Press, 1958.

Postscript   Johannes Climacus, pseud. *Concluding Unscientific Postscript to the Philosophical Fragments*. Translated by David F. Swenson and Walter Lowrie. Princeton, N. J.: Princeton University Press, 1941.

X^3 A 370 (example)   Following standard international practice, *Papirer* entries are cited by giving the volume in Roman numerals, the group-letter in capitals (A for journals, B for manuscripts and drafts, C for reading and study notes), and the specific entry number in Arabic numerals. If a volume has more than one part this is indicated by an Arabic numeral after the volume number and before the group letter. *Papirer* references always include the capital letter to indicate group and thus are never confused with the *Vaerker* references which never include letters.

CHAPTER ONE

THE CONFLICT BETWEEN PASSION AND REASON

The purpose of this chapter is to inquire into the distinction between passion and reason in some modern philosophies and into the views of passion which that division has suggested, as a preface to an examination of the concepts of passion and faith. The "conflict" between passion and reason, as it is traditionally called, is a notion which has been introduced to mark off a variety of features of some passion concepts and to link these features together in a systematic way. But if this division is taken as a general guide to the nature of the passions, the position of some (such as faith, hope, and love) is rendered extremely puzzling. One wonders whether these passions, too, share the liabilities attributed to the class as such--whether, for example, they are as passions unreasonable, passive, or even altogether chaotic. This chapter, then, has the preliminary task of looking into the source of our puzzlement here, and of asking how the postulation of a conflict between passion and reason influences the general picture of passion concepts.

The method will not be one of historical survey, but will proceed rather by selecting two kinds of position and two kinds of philosophical methodology to lead into the problematic which informs the philosophical theories.

A. Descartes and the Mechanism of the Passions

With the questions concerning the nature of the passions and of the relationship between passion and reason, as with so many other topics in modern philosophy, Descartes sets the stage. In his treatise "The Passions of the Soul," Descartes lays out his explanatory framework by drawing the now familiar, sharp distinction between "extended substance" or "body," and "thinking substance" or "soul." The body, which he typically calls "the bodily machine,"[1] operates according to the laws of

---

[1] René Descartes, "The Passions of the Soul," *The Philosophical Works of Descartes*, ed. Haldane and Ross, Vol. I (New York, 1955), e.g., Articles VI, VII, XIII, XVI, and XXXIV.

classical mechanics. The soul, on the other hand, is fully distinct from the body in nature and operation. We shall not go far astray if we think of it as a non-bodily non-machine; its attributes are "all that which is in us and which we cannot in any way conceive as possibly pertaining to a body."[2]

What is a passion? Of the two possibilities, thoughts or extended things, Descartes picks the former. Thoughts, in turn, are divided into two classes:

(1) The *actions* (that is, the desires out of which the soul acts directly on the pineal gland to set the body in motion); and

(2) The *passions*, which include the perceptions of objects, the perceptions of our internal states, and the "passions" in the narrower sense (joy, anger, and the like).[3]

This last class, the "passions of the soul," is defined as "the perceptions, feelings, or emotions of the soul which we relate specially to it, and which are caused, maintained, and fortified by some movement of the spirits."[4] Such passions are "perceptions" but of an unclear sort; they are a kind of feeling "received into the soul in the same way as are the objects of our outside senses."[5]

Actions and passions, acting and being acted on, pushing and being pushed--the dichotomy is so natural, especially to those who are fascinated by a mechanical model of mind, that it may seem well-nigh inevitable. And who would not be so inclined in the era of post-Copernican physics? As in the bodily realm there is action and reaction, so also in the non-bodily: thoughts are divided into those in which one acts (the desires) and those in which one is acted upon (of two classes, the perceptions and the emotions). Descartes did not create this view out of nothing, nor is it just an extrapolation from certain theories in physical science. It might be said to be embedded in many

---

[2]*Ibid.*, Article III, p. 332.

[3]*Ibid.*, Articles XVII-XXV, pp. 340-43.

[4]*Ibid.*, Article XXVII, p. 344.

[5]*Ibid.*, Article XXVIII, p. 344.

everyday locutions. But since Descartes did set the formal
terminology in which the questions about passion would be raised,
it was a fateful day for philosophy when he made clear, distinct,
and absolute the breach between actions and passions.

The way in which Descartes develops his notion about the
passions in terms of variations in the plumbing system of the
human physical plant may conceal from us the significance of the
philosophical move he has made. Talk about the pineal gland as
the locus for the conflict of passion and reason[6] sounds quaint
and unconvincing to modern ears. This apparent obsolescence is
unfortunate, for with the thesis that the "passions" are not
"actions" Descartes is in fact preparing the way for the modern
discussion of one of the most puzzling topics in philosophy of
mind. To enter into the context of this problem let us look
briefly at a way in which the question of the nature of the
passions arises.

We shall begin from some standard examples of the concept
of passion. Romeo loves Juliet. Well-meant advice, a feud, and
even death are unable to keep him from her. That's a passion.
Or take a headline: MAN, 42, FEARS DEATH, SLAYS FOUR ASSAILANTS.
Surely there is passion involved here, too. And besides these
cases which leap to mind, there are a great many others which
are covered by the term according to fairly common usage--situa-
tions involving anger, joy, regret, avarice, pride, hope, envy,
and others. Perhaps it is a sign of mean-spirited times that the
term today is apt to be restricted to extremely agitated emotions.
Philosophers of an earlier era spoke of the passions much more
broadly. They included many of the vices and virtues and allowed
for the full range of intensity, from the "grand passions" to the
fearful flicker of an eyelash and even (as in the case of hope)
where there might be no agitation at all.

Many philosophers have not been satisfied with the motley
collection of passions and their characteristics which we have
given. They have preferred to tidy them up, to find the *arche*
or at least to identify the genus and differentiae for the passions. For this purpose they have drawn on a number of rule-of-
thumb generalizations about what passions are and how they work.
For example:

---

[6]*Ibid.*, Articles XXXI-XXXVI, pp. 345-48.

(1) A passion is "passive"; it just happens to a person.
(2) It is a feeling of agitation.
(3) The person who has the passion has the only or at least a privileged position for knowing about it; and
(4) He always knows about it.
(5) It may be directed toward a special object, but that object is not essential to the description of it.
(6) It may involve certain kinds of behavior, but what these are is not integrally involved in the passion either.
(7) It is apt to make one go against his good judgment, to make an "emotional judgment."
(8) It involves no judgment at all, but just having the feeling.

The whole of this list ought not to be blamed on anyone, not even on the much-maligned "man on the street." Probably no one would maintain very long or very hard that love, joy, hope, and the rest just happen to someone in a strictly passive way (1), though the contrary idea, that one decides to do them, is perhaps even more unpalatable. Moreover, (7) and (8) are incompatible. There is no need to try to reconcile all the items on the list. Some passions are much better examples of one of the generalizations than others. Terror represents passivity (1) quite well, but it is hard to see what judgment (7) is involved--perhaps one about the danger inherent in the object of terror. Envy, on the other hand, could be called an "emotional judgment" (7) in a somewhat strained sense, but we blame the envious man and do not write off his emotion as something which just happened to him (1).

As a collection of generalities the list is vague, unorganized, incomplete, and rather uninteresting. Items in it first become philosophically important when they are appealed to in order to buttress a conceptual account of what passions are, how they function, or how they are related to "reason." That, at any rate, is a time-established way for philosophizing about the passions, and it is the route Descartes followed. The eight items on the list are mentioned here, not because they deserve by themselves special respect or treatment, but because they are among the main commonsense props for the viewpoints Descartes fathered, those theories which are often lumped together by contemporary philosophers as the "traditional view" on the passions.

B. The "Traditional View" on the Passions

As examples of the so-called traditional view we shall discuss two kinds of theories about the passions, the first of which was championed by Hume and the other by Spinoza.

1. The Regularity Theory

According to the simpler and commoner[7] viewpoint, a passion is something like an internal sensation, such as thirst, for example, or pain. The commonplace about passions stated in (2) is not at all surprising on this account, for a "feeling" of a special sort is just what a passion *ex hypothesi* is. All the rest of the factors in a description of passions--the object, the accompanying behavior, and the judgment about states of affairs (5, 6, and 8)--are incidental and inessential. Further, it is easy to see that if a passion is like thirst or pain, one has a right to expect that the person who has the passion, like the person in thirst or pain, will be the first and perhaps the only one to know about it, and in fact he will necessarily know about it (3). To try to talk about one's own unknown pain is to be unintelligible.

Of this theory about the passions Hume is a capable proponent. Descartes is often listed as the spokesman, probably because his presentation is clearly indefensible and thus invites

---

[7] In a general way the standpoint discussed in this section represents the spectrum of viewpoints which have, since Ryle, been criticized as the "traditional view" that the emotions are private, episodic events. But the label is a very vague one. Ryle (in *Concept of Mind* [New York, 1949], Chapter One) identifies the target as Descartes. Anthony Kenny (in *Action, Emotion, and Will* [London, 1963], pp. 1-28) with a more detailed investigation finds aspects of the standpoint in Descartes, Locke, and Hume. Pitcher (*Mind*, LXXIV [July, 1965], p. 326) singles out Hume and William James; while Bedford (in *Philosophy of Mind* [Englewood Cliffs, N.J., 1962], Chappell, ed., p. 110) picks Russell and McTaggert.

Since the search for a common source for these widely differing philosophies would be vast and probably fruitless, one primary example of the position, Hume, has been selected as representative. This approach has the advantage of allowing us room also to take up another, complementary viewpoint in the philosophical tradition, the position of Spinoza in the *Ethics*.

easy attack. Hume, however, presents the outcome of the identification of passions with sensations ("impressions") in a more extreme and a more consistent fashion.[8]

With Hume we see the effect of carrying Descartes' grouping of the passions with the sensations nearly to its extreme conclusion. The passions become almost purely "passive," in the sense that they are not something which a person does and for which he is responsible. Descartes' notion that passions are not actions is reinforced by Hume with his opposition to "the suppos'd pre-eminence of reason above passion,"[9] which is summed up in his famous dictum that "Reason is, and ought only to be the slave of the passions, and can never pretend to any other office than to serve and obey them."[10] Here Hume seems to be outlining the proposal that our passions be relied on more, our rational and dispassionate judgment less, in coming to conclusions. But he is not. Instead, he is making a basic conceptual

---

[8]Hume's consistency is shown in the way he does not hold both (7) and (8) but only (7).

As one might expect, the situation is a good deal more complex than can be easily summarized here. Hume divides the perceptions of the mind into two kinds, *ideas* and *impressions*, and the latter is further separated into the *original* and the *secondary* impressions (*Treatise* II, 1,1). The original impressions include the sensations, pains and pleasures; while the secondary impressions or impressions of reflection "proceed from some of the original ones, either immediately or by the interposition of its idea" (*ibid.*). Thus far, Hume has merely paralleled Descartes' distinction between the "passions" in the broad sense and the "passions" strictly so called. But Hume then goes on to distinguish between the "calm passions" (the sense of beauty and deformity) and the "violent passions" (the standard group of passions, including love and hatred, grief and joy).

In some sense or other Hume wants to identify the passions (along with everything else which may be present to the mind) as "perceptions": "To hate, to love, to think, to feel, to see; all this is nothing but to perceive" (*ibid.*, I, 2,6; p. 67). And he is willing, with some passions at least, to speak of them (in this case, pride and humility) as being "simple and uniform impressions" which cannot be defined but which are so common and easily identifiable that no one can make a mistake about them (*ibid.*, II, 1,2; p. 277). But what is being "perceived" by a passion--an external object, an idea of an external object, or an internal sensation--is difficult to state with surety, especially since Hume analyzes the different passions in an intricate variety of ways.

[9]*Ibid.*, II, 3,3; p. 413.

[10]*Ibid.*, II, 3,3; p. 415.

point which follows from his connecting the concept of passion with that of interior sensation. No more than with thirst or pain, he suggests, may one speak coherently of justifying them with reasons--they are events which happen to a person, not actions which one performs. His position both on the passions and on passion and reason comes out in a section following the well-known statement just quoted. The explanatory passage reads:

> A passion is an original existence, or, if you will, modification of existence, and contains not any representative quality, which renders it a copy of any other existence or modification. When I am angry, I am actually possest with the passion, and in that emotion have no more a reference to any other object, than when I am thirsty, or sick, or more than five foot high. 'Tis impossible, therefore, that this passion can be oppos'd by, or be contradictory to truth and reason; since this contradiction consists in the disagreement of ideas, consider'd as copies, with those objects, which they represent.[11]

What is maintained here is that a passion

(1) has no "representative quality"; it is not a "copy" or picture of anything else.

(2) It has no "reference to any other object"; that is, it has no intentional object or objects, and in this respect is not like, for example, thinking (which must be thinking *about* something), but rather like pain (which may or may not be directed toward anything in particular). And

(3) it is not opposed to reason, since reason has to do only with truth, and truth consists in the correspondence of an idea with the object of which it is a "copy."

This argument is revealing. The conclusion, (3), follows from (1), at least given Hume's theory of truth. But what of (2)? Hume tries by this denial of the intentionality of the passions to reinforce (1), but in fact he makes nonsense of the statement of his theory up to this point. For if the passions contain "no reference to any other object," how are we to explain that the passions arise out of a "prospect of pain or pleasure"

---

[11]*Ibid.*

from some objects or other, with the "consequent emotion of
aversion or propensity" toward these objects? Hume's quandary
here does not arise from a simple slip in reasoning. There is
a close conceptual link between the notion that passions have
intentional objects and the thesis that they are susceptible to
justification. Some philosophers would insist, against Hume,
that both hold true of the passions: when one fears, one necessarily fears something, and one may be expected to bring forth
grounds for the fear. Often the grounds one cites for the fear
will be simply a description of the intentional object. Likewise,
the confession that one's fear has no object will often (though
not always--for example with "nameless fears") imply that the
fear is groundless as well. But Hume, as we have seen, inter-
prets the passions on the model of the interior sensations, such
as thirst, of which neither intentionality nor susceptibility to
justification (in the sense in which knowledge claims are justified, at any rate) holds.[12]

2. The Rationalistic Theory

The Humean account which has been just examined begins
from a virtual identification of passions and interior sensations, and arrives at the conclusion that passions are not actions and therefore cannot be justified with reasons. They are
not actions, for which we are responsible, but regularities in
our behavior which take place. For this reason the Humean viewpoint has been labeled here the "regularity" theory of the passions.

A more complex and in certain respects a more satisfactory
theory on this topic is put forward by Spinoza, according to which
a passion consists of *both* the sensation of a bodily state *and*
the perception of that sensation (together with the idea of the

---

[12]Hume cites two minor exceptions to the principle that passions cannot be justified: (1) where the passion is founded on
the existence of an object which does not exist, and (2) where in
our passion we choose means insufficient to achieve our ends. All
other cases he dismisses abruptly: "Where a passion is neither
founded on false suppositions, nor chuses means insufficient for
the end, the understanding can neither justify nor condemn it.
'Tis not contrary to reason to prefer the destruction of the
whole world to the scratching of my finger" (*ibid.*, II, 3,3; p.
416).
The inadequacy of Hume's analysis has been noted by A. C.
Ewing in "The Justification of Emotions," *PASS* (1957), pp. 62-72,
and by George Pitcher, "Emotion," *Mind*, LXXIV (July, 1965), pp.
330-31.

The Traditional View

object toward which the passion is directed, its intentional object). The strength of Spinoza's theory comes just at that point at which we have criticized Hume, on the justification of passions. Spinoza provides a scheme within which the rationality of every passion can be evaluated, not just relative to this assumption or that, but in absolute quantitative terms according to the clarity and distinctness of the perception involved. Here, surely, is the ultimate example of a theory which proposes to evaluate precisely and conclusively the rationality of the passions. Accordingly, it may be called the "rationalistic" theory of the passions.

Spinoza's position on the relationship between mind and body is well known. Instead of viewing them as two independent substances, Spinoza posits one substance with two attributes, thought and extension. In this way the Cartesian split in man between mind and body is overcome; and the unity which has thus been found in human nature is taken to be basic to nature as a whole.

Within Spinoza's theory the concept of emotion plays a key role. In fact, the last three of the five books of the *Ethics* could well be read as a treatise on the nature and control of the passions.[13] Emotions are defined as "the modifications of the body by which the power of acting of the body itself is increased, diminished, helped, or hindered, together with the ideas of these modifications."[14] Together with this definition goes a principle

---

[13] This may be seen even in the titles of these chapters: "Of the Origin and Nature of the Emotions," "Of Human Bondage; or of the Strength of the Emotions," and "Of the Power of the Intellect; or of Human Freedom [from the emotions]."

[14] *Ethics*, ed. James Gutmann (New York, 1949), Book III, Definition III, p. 128. Later (Book III, p. 185) he supplements this with a "general definition of the emotions" as follows: "Emotion which is called *animi pathema* is a confused idea by which the mind affirms of its body, or any part of it, a greater or less power of existence than before; and this increase of power being given, the mind itself is determined to one particular thought rather than to another." In the explanation to this definition he accounts for the fact that "an emotion or passion of the mind *is a confused idea*" (italics his) by reminding us of his principle that "the mind suffers only insofar as it has inadequate or confused ideas."

From this definition it would appear that passions and emotions are essentially confused and productive of weakness. The one emotion which is an exception to the rule is the "intellectual love of God," in which the mind unconfusedly (cont...)

whose crucial importance can hardly be overemphasized: When the ideas of the body's modifications become more "adequate," that is to say, more "clear and distinct," then the body's power of acting is increased. In terms of emotions the person has become more full of "joy." On the other hand, to the extent that the ideas of bodily modifications become "inadequate" (unclear and indistinct), then the body is increasingly controlled by the "passions"[15] (that is, becomes more passive). As a person tends in this direction he is more and more overcome by "sorrow," "melancholy," and "pain."[16]

With this broad definition of emotion, together with the far-reaching principle correlating thoughts, actions, and emotions, the reason for the central position of the topic of emotion in the *Ethics* is evident. Spinoza is placing on one spectrum the perceptions, sensations, and abstract thought (all dealing with "ideas" in his terminology) ranging from the clearest perception to the dimmest sensation. In parallel with this scale he puts all cases where men act or are acted on. Alongside this, again, he lines up the emotions from those which give greatest joy to those which give the most sorrow and pain. And he says: As varies the clarity of the perception, so varies the degree of human activity and the amount of joy.

It is a bold stroke, broad and provocative in scope, worthy of the great seventeenth century metaphysician. He

---

contemplates God or Nature *sub specie aeternitatis*. In Book V, Proposition XXXIV (p. 273), he infers from the definition of emotion that "The mind is subject to emotions which are related to passions only so long as the body exists," and produces as a corollary the proposition that "no love except intellectual love is eternal" (p. 274). Within Spinoza's system this one emotion is not simply an exception to the general class of emotions, but its paradigm. But if one begins from usual cases of emotions—joy, envy, anger, and the like—and does not accept Spinoza's rationalistic schema, then the bodiless, atemporal state of the soul which Spinoza sets up as the standard looks very much out of place among the emotions. From a non-Spinozistic position "intellectual love" would best be described as a limiting case of emotion, at the boundary line where emotions become fully unconfused and therefore cease to be emotions. In any case the unconfused character of "intellectual love" does not ameliorate Spinoza's picture of the emotions but merely throws the sad state of all the other emotions into sharper relief.

[15]*Ibid.*, Book III, Proposition I, pp. 129-30, and esp. the Corollary, p. 130.

[16]*Ibid.*, Book III, Proposition XI, p. 137.

follows it up with a similar simplification within the concept of emotion itself. In addition to joy and sorrow he isolates one other basic emotion, desire[17] (also called "will" or "appetite"). Desire is identified with the very essence of a man, insofar as the man is conscious of his essence; for just as everything has a *conatus* toward existence, so also in the case of man is desire (that is, the effort to survive) of his very essence. Besides these three primary emotions Spinoza stresses that many emotions have intentional objects[18] and may be distinguished by these objects and by the way of relating to them. With these materials--primary emotions, objects, and ways of relating to objects--Spinoza builds up an impressive picture of the range of human emotions.[19]

The result of Spinoza's procedure is that many common notions about the emotions get quite turned about. The standard case of the rational man which he uses, the geometer, is not altogether implausible, and would have seemed more convincing to the seventeenth century than it does to us. But who of any age would have selected as a paradigm of *activity* the sage contemplating eternally clear and distinct truths? Still more perplexing is what he does with the standard examples of the passions, which in practically all cases turn out to be useless[20] and expendable, since if any bodily state were adequately (that is, clearly and distinctly) conceived it would for that very reason cease to be a passion.[21]

Is Spinoza recommending that all emotional life be replaced by the study of geometry? He does suggest that rational scrutiny will dismiss all those cases of the passions in which a

---

[17]*Ibid.*, Book III, Proposition IX, Note, pp. 136-37.

[18]E.g., with respect to the passions of love and hatred, in *ibid.*, Book V, Proposition II, pp. 255-56.

[19]E.g., in *ibid.*, Book III, Proposition LVI, pp. 169-71, and ff. to end of Book III.

[20]"It appears, therefore, that every desire which arises from an emotion wherein the mind is passive would be of no use if men could be led by reason." *Ibid.*, Book IV, Proposition LIX, p. 232. The only exception to this principle occurs in emotions wherein the mind is active, and of this kind of emotion there is only one adequate example, the "intellectual love of God." Cf. *supra*, footnote 14.

[21]*Ibid.*, Book V, Proposition III, p. 256.

man is swept away by some feeling or another and which vary from one man to the next and within one man from one moment to another.[22] And this is an extremely disconcerting statement, since changeableness and variation from person to person are crucial characteristics of practically any emotion one can imagine. But Spinoza saves the class of emotions from utter annihilation by suggesting that there are emotions which do not fall under the ban. There are modifications of one's bodily states, and ideas of those states, which follow from man's essential nature, and in these emotions men are at one with each other and in harmony.[23] The true paradigm of emotion is to be found where men conceive of themselves and their actions *sub specie aeternitatis* with the "intellectual love of God."[24] It will be objected by the non-Spinozist that this so-called paradigm is wildly atypical of emotions and might well be ruled out of the emotions camp altogether; but this case is for Spinoza the only kind of emotion which can altogether pass the test of rationality.

Spinoza's *Ethics* presents a theory of the passions which is at the same time helpful and yet disconcerting. Many of his theses are a definite improvement on Descartes and the "regularity" theory. With Spinoza there is a level of awareness of the importance of the intentionality of emotions, the cognitive element in emotion, and the justification of emotions, which is lacking in Descartes and Hume. But the main scheme which he puts forward for the justification of emotions is such an impossible one as to cast the whole enterprise into disrepute. For what he does in effect is to agree with Descartes that the passions are some kind of sensation or perception, and then to set up a "justification" procedure which is appropriate only to sensations and perceptions, namely, the clarity and distinctness of the representation. We may applaud his interest in treating of the justification of emotions, and we will find many individual analyses of emotions which are subtly carried through despite the quantitative scheme he has imposed, but the scheme itself will draw cheers from few people. Again, the reader may well be impressed

---

[22] *Ibid.*, Book IV, Proposition XXXIV, pp. 209-10.

[23] *Ibid.*, Book IV, Propositions XXXV and XXXVI, pp. 211-13.

[24] *Ibid.*, Book V, Propositions XXXI-XXXIII, pp. 272-73.

by the moving portrayal he gives us of the "intellectual love of
God," and be delighted and relieved that some philosopher at
least has seen fit to treat of an emotion beside the stock examples, fear or anger, which lend themselves so deceptively easily
to a mechanical model. But who will follow him (who would dare?)
when he proposes that all changeable human passions be subjugated,
and that the philosopher should increasingly devote himself to the
dispassionate contemplation of what is eternally and necessarily
true? The joy at the first glow of sunrise and the faint songs
of the birds, the righteous indignation of the prophet, the tenderness of romantic love--all these must be left behind. Many a
would-be disciple of Spinoza will turn away sorrowful when faced
with a demand like that.

Descartes puts forward the thesis that passions are not
actions and he is seconded strongly by Hume. Spinoza's work,
puzzling as it is, opens the possibility that some emotions at
least may be considered as actions, which need to be justified
and for which we may be held responsible. The claim which Spinoza
makes is much more than this and the achievement, we have maintained, is much less. Nevertheless, if he has taught us only that
much, what he has said is important.

C. Ordinary Language Theories

Let us turn from the classical theories of the passions
to contemporary treatments of the topic, and in particular those
in the kind of analytic philosophy inspired by Wittgenstein.
Within this later tradition there is an insistence on the conceptual as opposed to empirical character of philosophical inquiry. As clues to the subtle variations among concepts which
underlie philosophical disputes, these modern thinkers frequently
turn to the conceptual distinctions embedded in non-philosophical
or "ordinary" language.[25] Is there within the analytic tradition
a persistence of the philosophical problems which perplexed
Descartes, Spinoza, and Hume? To answer this question we shall
examine the passion and reason problematic as it arises in the
writing of three spokesmen of the contemporary tradition, Gilbert
Ryle, Errol Bedford, and Richard Peters.

---

[25]See *infra*, footnote 36.

1. Ryle: Emotions as Dispositions

Ryle occupies a place within the current discussion of emotion concepts similar to that of Descartes in an earlier century: without being the originator of the viewpoint he represents, Ryle has largely succeeded in formulating the questions and setting the technical terminology for other thinkers. The analogy with Descartes extends to the results of their efforts. Just as there were few philosophers after Descartes who could accept all the consequences of his sharp disjunction between mind and matter, especially when talking about the passions, so also many of those who follow Ryle most closely are apt to disagree with him most vehemently in results. As there were Cartesians there are Ryleans, but in neither case would the father have recognized the legitimacy of all his offspring.

Of the two directions of theory on the passions, the "regularity" and the "rationalistic" views, Ryle's position on the issue of passion versus reason corresponds more closely to the former, which we have identified with Descartes and Hume. But it is also primarily against these two thinkers and what he calls the "Cartesian myth" that Ryle directs his attack. His argument is that the Cartesian position mistakenly identifies emotions as "episodic" and isolated sensations; and that, while one cannot rule such a view out of court, it is possible to show by an examination of our ordinary-language emotion vocabulary that the senses of "emotion" in which the term identifies an episodic feeling such as thrills, twinges, pangs, throbs, wrenches, itches, and the like[26] are quite atypical of the broad spectrum of uses

---

[26] Gilbert Ryle, *The Concept of Mind* (New York, 1949), pp. 83-84. In an article in *PQ*, I (April, 1951), pp. 193-205, Ryle shows that the term "feeling" has at least seven different uses in English, of which the sense which suggests aches and twinges is only one. His list is: (1) "perceptual use," where we feel with our fingers or feel cold; (2) the "explanatory use," in which one "feels for" one's matches or "feels" someone's pulse; (3) the mock-use of (1), where one "feels as if" one perceives something; (4) aches, tickles, and other local or pervasive discomforts (this is the sense which usually serves as paradigm for Descartes' usage); (5) feel a general condition, as in "feel sleepy"; (6) "feel that" something is the case; (7) "feel like" doing something. To take one sense of the term, such as (4), as our guide in a philosophical analysis is to run the risk of overlooking the rich variety of functions of the concept.
On this range of the concept of feeling, cf. William P. Alston, "Feelings," *PR*, LXXVIII (January, 1969), pp. 3-34.

of the term, and particularly those uses with which philosophers are most concerned.

Ryle's positive account of emotion treats it as universally "dispositional" (with the exception of twinges, and the like, as just noted) rather than episodic. That is to say, an emotion is not identified with the continued presence of a certain distinctive feeling, but rather with the disposition to feel, to act, and to speak in certain characteristic ways if the right conditions obtain. To say that someone is jealous of his wife is not to say that he necessarily has at every moment a special jealous feeling,[27] but rather that he tends under certain circumstances, such as when he hears her praised by other men, to speak sharply, to have pangs of jealousy, to take steps to remove the cause of affront--and perhaps, though not necessarily, all three of these. The term "disposition"[28] here is drawn from a usage in the physical sciences to describe concepts such as that of solubility. Just as to say that sugar is soluble is not to make any categorical statement about the state of the sugar at any moment, but rather the hypothetical statement that *if* the sugar is placed in water it will dissolve, so to say that someone is jealous does not mean that he at each moment feels a certain way, but that *if* certain occasions arise he will lash out, and so forth.[29]

---

[27]Nor is it to say that he has this feeling but does not know it; the notion of a feeling of which one is not aware can be an extremely paradoxical one, if by "feeling" one understands such states as tickles and twinges.

[28]*Concept of Mind*, pp. 43-44, 88-89.

[29]The limitations of this analogy between the concept of disposition in physical science and that in human behavior have been pointed out by Stuart Hampshire in an article in *Analysis*, XIV, No. 1 (October, 1953), pp. 5-11. A physical disposition (such as being soluble in *aqua regia*) differs from a disposition in human behavior (such as being generous) in that: (1) to ascribe the disposition of solubility does not carry the implication that the substance has ever been so dissolved; (2) a disposition of solubility does not have to manifest itself more or less continuously over a period of time; and (3) a disposition of solubility must show itself in "specific and statable reactions" of a determinate sort; whereas none of these characteristics hold true, at least to the same extent, of a disposition toward generosity (pp. 7-8). Hampshire prefers to speak of the ascription of generosity as the offering in categorical statements of an interpretive summary of the person's past behavior, rather than the giving of hypothetical statements about what he may do. A comment similar to Hampshire's first distinction is made by Erik Götlind in (cont...)

Failure to recognize that there are dispositional and for the most part publicly accessible factors by which emotions are identified would lead, Ryle fears, to the positing of "occult" and

---

his *Three Theories of Emotion* (Lund, 1958), p. 125, when he observes that it makes sense to say of a sort of glass that it is brittle though it has never been struck, but it does not "make the same good sense to say about a dead person that he was very vain, but he never showed any sign of vanity for lack of circumstances which would have revealed his true character."

Hampshire also criticizes Ryle's treatment of dispositions in his review of the *Concept of Mind*, *Mind*, LIX (April, 1950), pp. 244-49. More recently, in his inaugural address at the University of London (25 October 1960) entitled "Feeling and Expression," he has elaborated an account of the place of dispositions in emotions alternative to that of Ryle. In Hampshire's treatment, feelings are identified as the "residual" parts (p. 9) or "interiorizations" (p. 16) of what he calls the "natural expression" of a emotion. Thus the "fundamental dispositions that constitute a standard of normality" for the emotion of anger, for example, are those of the angry man who, being provoked, immediately attacks; but when for various reasons the man begins to inhibit the expression of his feelings all that remains is a "residual" scowl. In this way Hampshire is able to preserve a close tie between behavioral dispositions and, e.g., "the inner movement of the mind" (p. 17). But quite apart from certain unclarities in this theory (can one independently identify this "inner movement," for example?) there are obvious limitations for the application for the theory. John Benson in "Emotion and Expression," *PR*, LXXVI (July, 1967), p. 345, brings up the instance of raising an eyebrow and asks of what fully fledged action it is residual. Although it may be residual we cannot identify the source, and so this cannot be how we come to understand the gesture.

Ryle's discussion of dispositions has been defended against Hampshire's *Analysis* critique by G. N. Bird and Alan R. White. Bird ("Mr. Hampshire on Dispositions," *Analysis*, XIV, No. 4 [March, 1954], pp. 100-02) gives strong arguments to show that the distinction between physical dispositions and dispositions toward human behavior is not as sharp as Hampshire insists. White ("Mr. Hampshire and Professor Ryle on Dispositions," *Analysis*, XIV, No. 5 [April, 1954], pp. 110-14) gives evidence from the *Concept of Mind* to show that Ryle noted and allowed for the very differences between kinds of dispositions which Hampshire discusses. Moreover, White says, the two views of dispositions are complementary, not contrary, since statements about human dispositions serve both the function Hampshire calls attention to, of summarizing a person's past behavior, and the use Ryle points to, of predicting what the person may do under certain circumstances. White's citations are convincing; but in fairness to Hampshire it should be noted that although Ryle does make such qualifications, in his typically offhand manner, the reader of the *Concept of Mind* is apt to get the impression that the analogy between the concept of disposition in physical science and that in psychology is much closer than either White or Hampshire would maintain.

non-dispositional feelings--to which no one, not even the person involved, has sure access--as the criteria for the application of emotion concepts.

When Ryle attempts to apply his dispositional view of emotion concepts generally, however, he runs into severe difficulties which are reminiscent of those which we have examined in the Cartesian and Humean theories he is criticizing. All goes well with the treatment of moods as dispositions, in this respect at least. But when he comes to motives, which are the crucial case for the passion/reason question, he tries valiantly but unsuccessfully to show that they are dispositional concepts. Ryle's standard example is "He boasted from vanity." To say that the motive for his boasting was vanity, he says, is to explain his action by citing a "reason," that is, a law-like proposition which states his general disposition to act in vain ways. He is, as in the case of any other motive

> inclined to do certain sorts of things, make certain sorts of plans, indulge in certain sorts of daydreams and also, of course, in certain situations to feel certain sorts of feelings. To say that he did something from that motive is to say that this action, done in its particular circumstances, was just the sort of thing that that was an inclination to do. It is to say "he *would* do that."[30]

But there are obvious difficulties with this account of motives. One could not ascribe a motive to a first offender in boasting or other forms of vanity but would have to wait until his vanity became a marked trait of character. By the same token, there would be no way to speak of a motive which was out of character. If a given action, boasting, did not fit in with a trend of the past vain behavior of the man, we should have to conclude that his motive in boasting was not vanity after all, and would be hard put to decide what other motive it might be.[31]

And what a remarkably unilluminating explanation this reason "He boasted from vanity" turns out to be! "Why did he boast?" "Because that's the sort of thing he always does, given the opportunity. He *would* do that." Imagine saying to someone:

---

[30] *Concept of Mind*, pp. 92-93.

[31] Cf. G. E. M. Anscombe, *Intention* (Oxford, 1958), p. 21, and Kenny, *Action, Emotion and Will* (London, 1963), p. 77.

Why did you boast? and getting the reply: I always do that whenever I get a chance. Our surprise would not be at the unusual candor about his motives, but rather that he would propose that as a statement about motives at all. Or try another example very close to Ryle's: "He boasted from boastfulness." If motives were inclinations this should be a perfectly good one, tailor-made to explain the action. We would understand the boastful action by seeing it as just one sample of a boastful trend. But anyone who said "Oh yes, I know what his motive for boasting was--boastfulness!" would just be making a bad joke.

What seems to have misled Ryle here is an ambiguity in that deceptive word "reason." There is a sense in which citing his past tendency to boast gives the "reason" for his action, and one does well when he, like Ryle, distinguishes "reason" in this sense from the citation of a particular incident in the past as the "cause" of his boasting. This is the difference between pointing to an *inclination* and pointing to an *incident* as the explanation, and Ryle calls this the difference between explaining by a "reason" and explaining by a "cause." But there is another use of "reason" altogether involved when one provides the *motive* for an action. One is not just pointing to a past behavior trend which may continue into the future, but giving a way of at least partly *justifying* the action. One does this by pointing not to an incident, as with a cause, or to a trend, as with an inclination-reason, but often to some factor or thing which will account for the goal or purpose he had in view.[32]

The confusion here is subtle and not easy to detect. It is quite true that inclinations and moods both involve purpose, at least on occasion. There are inclinations toward purposive behavior and moods in which one tends to act purposively. Moreover, it is often helpful to cite the approximate temperament

---

[32]Ryle is not denying that inclinations can be purposive. At one point he even states that "An inclination is a certain sort of proneness or readiness to do certain sorts of things on purpose" (*Concept of Mind*, p. 106). (This is surely too strong, since there are inclinations which are not "on purpose.")

What Ryle is denying is that stating a motive is doing anything more than ascribing a kind of regularity to a behavior trend, whether purposive or not. A motive does not give the rationale for an action or appraise it, but merely summarizes the trend and leads us to expect similar behavior in the future.

or mood—an inclination toward vanity, for example, or a mood of cheerfulness—when asked the "reason," in one sense, for certain actions. (Q: Why are you singing in the shower? A: I'm just in a cheerful mood, that's all.) And motives, too, involve purposive action and give the "reason" for action. But they give the reason in a quite different way from inclinations or moods. By and large it makes perfectly good sense, in fact, to ask for the motive for an inclination, for example, the tendency to boast. One might say that the motive for this tendency is his pride in his country, his hope to impress his wife, his desire to sell some merchandise, or any number of other reasons. Ryle's example is a bit atypical in this respect. One cannot speak of a motive for vanity, because no one would try to be vain, nor for that matter, of a motive for being humble, because trying to be humble simply creates smugness. But one can very well give motives for other such traits, such as courage and self-control.

The same difficulty as we have been discussing concerning Ryle's use of "reason" arises also with respect to the accompanying concept of explanation. Inclinations and moods, in their quite different ways, both provide explanations for certain sorts of behavior, and they do this by showing that the behavior is part of a distinctive and consistent pattern of actions. But giving the motives does something else than this: it states the rationale for the actions. There are inclinations toward action which are "on purpose," but the purposes for these inclinations are motives (certainly not some sort of higher order inclinations!). The distinction is simply between explanations which identify *what* a set of actions, feelings, etc., is by subsuming it under a law; and explanations which point out *why* an action or set of actions is undertaken or *why* one willingly takes on the character traits which make one, for example, courageous.[33]

This distinction ought not, of course, to be made overly sharp. The number of kinds of explanations is only limited by the number of kinds of human curiosities which can be satisfied, and one should not expect to find neat borderlines when handling concepts of activities so various and complex. Ryle's example represents a sort of boundary line case here, which makes it

---

[33]On motives and kinds of explanation see Alan R. White, *The Philosophy of Mind* (New York, 1967), pp. 134-42, esp. p. 140.

unfortunate that Ryle took it as a paradigm. It is just possible that someone might give as the motive for his boasting that he has always boasted before and acted in generally vain ways and he saw no reason to change now. And then people might say of him, wagging their heads in dismay: He just keeps boasting and boasting, and the only "reason" for it seems to be that he's always boasted before.[34]

From what has been said it will be seen that Ryle, in attempting to exorcize Cartesian ghosts, is yet haunted by their near relation, the spectre of Hume. Although the dispositional theory of emotions avoids certain difficulties in the "traditional view" (notably the postulating of a strange privacy of emotions and the incorrigibility of reports about them), it presents other problems which are very similar to those found in Descartes and Hume.[35] How can simply identifying *either* an episode *or* a disposition as an emotion be a way of justifying or criticizing that episode or disposition, as happens when we say either is an instance, for example, of courage or of cowardice? Ryle, no less than those he criticizes, fails to give a satisfactory account of the way in which certain uses of emotion terms do not merely report what has happened but interpret why it happened. And Ryle's shortcoming here is not, as has sometimes been suggested,[36] that

---

[34] But even here one would be more apt to say that his actions were explained by a habit than by a motive.
   The plausibility of Ryle's account arises from the fact that we do frequently demand that there be a certain degree of regularity in a person's actions before we confidently ascribe a motive for what he does; but even in these cases Ryle is mistaken in asserting that ascribing the motive consists simply in pointing to the regularity involved.

[35] It is the parts of the *Concept of Mind* such as the treatment of motives as tendencies toward kinds of behavior which lend what credence there is to the frequent accusation that Ryle falls into a new kind of "behaviorism." The term is applied to Ryle, for example, by Dickinson S. Miller in "'Descartes' Myth' and Professor Ryle's Fallacy," *JP*, XLVIII (April 26, 1951), p. 272; by Morris Weitz in "Professor Ryle's 'Logical Behaviorism'," *JP*, XLVIII (April 26, 1951), pp. 297-301; and by Margaret MacDonald in "Professor Ryle on the Concept of Mind," *PR*, LX (1951), p. 85 (with a sharp distinction from classical behaviorism, as "logical or analytical behaviorism").

[36] Erik Götlind, in *Three Theories of Emotions: Some Views of Philosophical Method* (Lund, 1958), pp. 147-48, attributes the shortcomings of Ryle's theory of emotions to the way he restricts himself to ordinary language and thus has no way (cont...)

he has followed ordinary language too closely; for the distinctions which he needs are those to which we have been appealing in common parlance, but which his universal application of the disposition notion will not permit him to observe.

2. Bedford: Emotions as Appraisals

That the use of ordinary-language methodology does not by itself lead to Ryle's dispositional analysis of emotion concepts is shown by the presence of another position in contemporary analytic philosophy, outlined by Errol Bedford,[37] which stresses the evaluative side of these concepts and in this way shows analogies to the Spinozistic presentation.

Bedford agrees with Ryle's critique of the view that emotions are private mental episodes, but not with his positive account of emotion concepts. A dispositional account of a person's behavior will indeed give some sort of explanation of what he does, Bedford says, but no combination of sentences about someone's behavior--categorical (of episodes) or hypothetical (of dispositions or tendencies to action)--no matter how long or complex, will do what an emotion statement does. Such a description can only provide a necessary condition for ascribing an emotion to someone; for the necessary and sufficient conditions something else is required than the apparatus which either Ryle or the traditional theory provides.[38]

---

of dealing with psychological and psychiatric phenomena and their relation to everyday experience. But this criticism misses Ryle's point. In his essay on "Ordinary Language" (in *Ordinary Language*, ed. V. C. Chappell [Englewood Cliffs, N. J., 1964]), Ryle makes clear that the opposite of "ordinary" language is not "technical" language but "philosophers' jargon" and "formalism" (p. 38). There are reasons why philosophers will occasionally draw on technical terms from other fields (p. 36) and other reasons why they should be cautious in this respect (p. 37); but the purpose of the appeal to ordinary language is neither to condemn nor to allow technical language, but rather to appeal from language whose proprieties are unclear (often because the terms were coined simply to "solve" philosophical puzzles) to those linguistic usages (technical or otherwise) which we have learned to handle easily.

[37]"Emotions," reprinted in *The Philosophy of Mind*, ed. V. C. Chappell (Englewood Cliffs, N. J., 1962), pp. 110-26.

[38]Bedford does sometimes appear to be making a more sweeping claim than this, and to deny that emotions necessarily involve feelings at all. He is opposed, he says, to the "traditional theory of the emotions" according to which "an emotion (cont...)

Two more factors are involved, according to Bedford:

(1) that the emotions are put into a social or interpersonal context; and
(2) that "emotion words explain by giving one sort of reason for an action, i.e., by giving a justification, or partial justification, for it."[39]

Despite the fact that these two are closely interrelated, let us look at them in turn, using one of Bedford's examples, the distinction between the emotions of embarrassment and of shame.

> The behavior of an embarrassed man is often not noticeably different from that of one who is ashamed; but there is an important difference between the respective situations they are in. In a newspaper article last year, Mr. Peter Davies, the publisher, was said to be "to his embarrassment" the original of Peter Pan. The embarrassment is understandable, and the epithet appropriate, whether the application is correct or not. Yet we can say at once that if the writer of the article had alleged that Mr. Davies was "to his shame" the original of Peter Pan, this would have been incorrect; it is scarcely conceivable that it could be true. The reason for this is obvious, and it is logical, not psychological, since it has nothing to do with

---

is a feeling, or at least an experience of a special type which involves a feeling" (p. 110). This leaves him open to correction from Moreland Perkins ("Emotion and Feeling," *PR*, LXXV [April, 1966], pp. 139-60), who argues that there is at least "one *concept* of emotion that differs from the concept Bedford has analyzed" (p. 151, italics in original), according to which to have an emotion necessarily involves having certain feelings.

But Bedford's argument is on the whole more modest than the above statements suggest. He is opposed to the view that the names for emotions are names for specific feelings (pp. 110-11), and he insists "that an emotion is not any sort of experience or process" (p. 110 note); he does not think "that expressions such as 'is angry' gain their *whole* meaning from an indirect reference that they make to experience, and can *only* be defined in terms of feelings" (p. 111, italics mine), or that "the *primary* function of these statements is to communicate psychological facts" (p. 122, italics mine).

Taken in the latter way Bedford's article need not contradict Perkins' contention that emotions involve some sort of feeling. Bedford would only be against the identification of emotions with specific feelings. What the primary function of the concept emotion is would still be in dispute perhaps, but with a concept as broad as this one there is surely room for a number of different emphases.

[39] Bedford, "Emotions," pp. 125-26.

Mr. Davies' behavior, still less with his feelings. It is simply that the fact that Barrie modeled Peter Pan on him is not his *fault*--it was not due to an act of his, and there is nothing reprehensible about it anyway.[40]

What does Ryle's dispositional treatment leave out? First, there is the interpersonal factor. Without an indication of the social context, no combination of statements about actions, feelings, or behavior trends will be enough by itself to identify the emotion.[41] Second, there is the evaluative aspect of emotions. One task, indeed the primary task, of ascriptions of emotion is to offer an appraisal or criticism of the situation described.[42] In terms of Bedford's example, the judgment is that it was an unpleasant and regrettable situation but that it was not his fault (in the case of embarrassment) or that it was his fault (in the case of shame). By offering an appraisal, emotion terms justify or partially justify the action which one takes.[43]

In effect, the two factors which Bedford finds to be left out of the dispositional theory are so closely related as to be almost indistinguishable. For it is within the context of social and political institutions that the moral appraisals of behavior in emotion statements are delivered; and it is to other people that we justify our actions by motive statements such as "because I was ashamed" or "because I was embarrassed."[44] By assimilating motives to dispositional concepts such as inclinations, then, Ryle has committed a kind of "category mistake" with regard to emotion concepts: he has treated these concepts as descriptions rather than "logically higher"[45] *interpretations* of descriptions.

---

[40] *Ibid.*, p. 116.

[41] *Ibid.*, p. 125.

[42] *Ibid.*, pp. 115, 119, 122.

[43] *Ibid.*, p. 126.

[44] "Emotion concepts, I have argued, are not purely psychological: they presuppose concepts of social relationships and institutions, and concepts belonging to systems of judgment, moral, aesthetic, and legal. In using emotion words we are able, therefore, to relate behavior to the complex background in which it is enacted, and so to make human actions intelligible." *Ibid.*

[45] *Ibid.*, p. 115 footnote.

3. Peters: Emotions as Distortions

Bedford's approach to the analysis of emotion is carried a step further by Richard Peters, who employs a scheme which is more comprehensive and, perhaps in virtue of this, less clear than that of Bedford.

Against Ryle, Peters insists that motives are not a species in the genus of emotions; but the fallacy is not that Ryle has his taxonomy wrong but that the question is not a taxonomical one. Emotion terms, he asserts, "are not classificatory ones; they are rather terms which are used to relate states of mind such as fear, anger, jealousy to distinctive frames of reference, those of activity and passivity."[46]

Although Peters does not recognize the matter, it is evident that this criticism of Ryle owes more to Bedford than the different terminology lets us easily see. Substitute Bedford's "not informative" for Peters' "not classificatory" (which are more or less equivalent, because the way in which these terms are supposed to be informative is by classifying an emotion under the appropriate heading), and then substitute Bedford's "higher order explanatory context" for Peters' "distinctive frames of reference," and the two arguments will be close to identical.

Despite this similarity of structure, however, there is a significant difference; for where Bedford has one second-level interpretive schema for appraising emotional dispositions and episodes, Peters has two, which he calls the "explanatory frameworks" of activity and passivity. What Bedford has specified as *emotion* judgments are not that at all, according to Peters, but are appraisals of *motive* which fit into the activity framework (they are motives for actions).[47] Those judgments which may properly be called "emotional," on the other hand, serve another and distinctive function which fits into a passivity model (they are, to use the traditional term, "passions").[48]

---

[46] Richard Peters, "Emotions and the Category of Passivity," *PAS*, LXII (1961-62), p. 120.

[47] Peters (*ibid.*, p. 120) footnotes his treatment of motives to Chapter Two of his book, *The Concept of Motivation* (London, 1958). The reference is presumably to p. 33 of that chapter, where he says that motives are only one kind of reason for an action, since we do not say that a reason is a motive unless it departs from the customary rules for the action.

[48] "Emotions and the Category of Passivity," pp. 120-21.

As a clue to the special function of the term "emotion" Peters looks to the "standard uses of the term" and discovers that these differ widely from the technical usage:

> The phrases in which the term "emotion" and its derivatives are not only natural but also indispensable are when we speak of judgments being disturbed, clouded, or warped by emotion, of people as being not properly in control of their emotions, being subject to gusts of emotion, being emotionally perturbed, upset, involved, excited, biased, and exhausted. In a similar vein we speak of emotional outbursts, reactions, upheavals, and women. The suggestion in such cases is always that something comes over people when they consider a situation in a certain kind of light. "Emotion," in the standard use of the term rather than in that coined by philosophers and psychologists, is used to suggest mists on our mental windscreen rather than straightforward judgments.[49]

In short, the distinctive character of "emotion" in its standard uses is that it marks appraisals which are distorted by feelings. With regard to behavior (which is, however, only loosely connected with emotions on Peters' view) the effect of emotions may be either to disrupt or to enhance what we do, but on our judgments the intrusion of emotions can apparently only work harm, so that "if we say that a judgment is an expression of emotion we are suggesting that it is a pretty poor sort of judgment."[50]

By following this understanding of "emotion" Peters is able to make a fairly sharp distinction between motives and emotions on the basis of what he at one point calls the two "models" of activity and passivity.

(1) Motives, on the one hand, are definite and realistic appraisals of situations, which explain by giving one sort of reason for a man's actions. In this way we account for a man's actions and performances by applying an "activity model" for the justification of the actions: "Assessment of the situations in accordance with reality criteria (e.g., those involved in perceiving and remembering) would be presupposed together with the grasp of means and ends which conform to standards of efficiency and social appropriateness."[51]

---

[49]*Ibid.*, p. 119.

[50]*Ibid.*, p. 120. Cf. *infra*, footnote 52.

[51]*Ibid.*, p. 133.

(2) Emotional appraisals, on the other hand, are unreliable as judgments, and the explanation they give does not clarify a man's grounds for his actions, but instead accounts for the distorted and mistaken judgments he makes about his actions. For emotions Peters offers what he calls the "passivity model" (so called because it does not deal with the way one acts but with the way one is affected by certain situations).

> The passivity model would explain departures from actions and performances (e.g., characteristic errors and distortions of thought, perception and memory, motor slips and break-downs) and goings-on like dreaming and hysteria which do not rank as performances or actions at all. It would also explain the enhancement and facilitation of such performances in various ways if they followed the lines of what was wished for.[52]

---

[52]*Ibid.* The interpretation of Peters in this essay, saying that he makes the characteristic feature of emotions to be the distortion of judgments, appears to run counter to several remarks he makes about emotions as the "enhancement," "facilitation," or "heightening" of our powers (*ibid.*, pp. 122, 125, 129, 133). But since he insists that the "distinctive" use of the concept of emotion comes in the distortion of judgment, he could certainly not be speaking in these places of the enhancement of *judgments*--at least, not directly--but is perhaps best understood as referring to the facilitation of certain kinds of physical processes. (The only passage which would go against this interpretation is point vi, on p. 129, where he speaks of "cognitive performances," but all the other examples in this passage suggest that an increase in certain physiological reactions is what he has chiefly in mind.)

Emotions, he says, do not assist us in forming good judgments, though they may help us execute our decisions; there are "gusts of emotion" which "speed us on our way" (pp. 121-22). Indeed, emotions are tied by him to a magical view of the world (p. 131) and are only loosely connected with purposive behavior or with a grasp of reality which would permit one to take practical steps.

The "standard use" of the term "emotion," Peters writes, is "to suggest mists on our mental windscreen rather than straightforward judgments" (p. 119). Following this metaphor, one might say that emotions may (or may not) tune up the engine, tighten the brakes, or in any other way "enhance" the operation of every other part of the car except the windshield wiper. The result of such enhancement may improve the driving in particular cases, but only accidentally; it may help on occasion to have tighter brakes, but since one will not be able to tell accurately through the foggy windshield when to brake, it will be only coincidentally that the prompt functioning of the brakes helps the driving. The prudent driver will clear the mists off his windshield; and the wise man will take all possible steps to avoid letting emotions play any part in the formation of his judgments.

On the basis of this distinction motives are distinguished from emotions in the following way: motives provide one kind of reason for actions; emotions give one kind of account of the causes for our lapses from reasonable action. Since motives are cognitive perhaps it would be best to call emotions anti-cognitive, because they are the sources for many of the breakdowns of our rational appraisals of situations.

Activity and Passivity: How sharp is the division between the two frameworks? Peters certainly believes that he is able to sort out the two kinds of cases, and from the way in which he does this he indicates that the clues to the correct procedure are linguistic ones. When a person is said to act "out of" fear, fear stands as a motive and thus gives a reason for his actions, while when he is said to act "in" fear, fear is simply the manner of the action and does not give the reason for which the action is performed.

Does this distinction hold? There is a difference in emphasis between the two cases, with more stress in the first case on the reason and in the second on the manner of the action. But the cleft is not at all absolute. What seems to be the case is that both "out of fear" and "in fear" are motives and both are emotions in Peters' senses of the terms. Would we say of the motive statement "out of fear" that it did *not* tell us that the person was "overcome," "disturbed," or "invigorated" by fear? Yet all of these terms are supposed to show our passivity and thus belong to the emotion framework. And would we say of the person who fled "in fear" of the approaching disaster that we did *not* know the reason but only the fearful manner of his flight? Of course not; we know very well what his reason was, just as well as we would if we were told he fled "out of fear."

Peters is willing to grant that there may be occasions on which one will act both "out of fear" and "in fear"--occasions, that is, where one has not only a reason to flee in fear one direction, but is also passively thrust in that direction by overpowering feelings. And he thinks it is "very nice when such gusts of emotions, as it were, speed us on our way rather than deflect us from our path."[53] But can one find clear or "standard cases" when one flees "out of fear" but not "in fear" or

---

[53]*Ibid.*, pp. 121-22.

vice versa? Peters finds the conjunction of these two a "nice" exception; but what seems rather the case is that the exceptions crowd out the rule.

The reason for the failure of our search is not, however, a contingent matter but is built into the concepts themselves. It has to do with the way the concept of fear is related to feelings. When one ascribes fear to someone one does not attribute to him a certain separately identifiable episode of fear-feeling which makes up the emotion. This much at least we have learned from Ryle and Bedford. *Part* of what we do expect of the person, however, is a disposition to behave in certain ways such as flight, if given the opportunity, and to feel certain sensations such as shivers running up and down one's spine. Bedford insists rightly that to say that an emotion involves a disposition in this way is not to give a full explanation of its logic. But it is correct as far as it goes, and dare not be omitted. And the distinctive dispositions of fear characterize fear no matter what explanatory framework they are placed within. Accordingly, when we cite fear as a motive in Peters' sense (and thus place it in the activity model) we do not thereby only give a reason (fear of x) for his actions, but also indicate the disposition of the person in question to have certain feelings--to be overcome, disturbed, and invigorated by these feelings in fact. Moreover, because feelings of this sort are not something we do--we do not produce the chill in the spine, we simply have it--these feelings are prime candidates for Peters' passivity model. As a result, *any* motive explanation of an action by means of a mental state such as fear which involves feelings is going to require *both* the activity and the passivity model at the same time. With cases where motive explanations are inappropriate, this is not necessarily true. One can easily imagine situations where one is so suddenly and completely overcome by fear--paralyzed by it in fact--that one cannot speak of an action having a reason, since there is no action involved but only an involuntary reaction. But this sort of instance is by no means a standard one, or else our logic of emotion terms would be far different from the one it is.

This close connection between the active and passive frameworks suggests that Peters' sharp distinction between them cannot be maintained in concrete cases. May one then suggest a looser, overlapping relationship between motives and emotions? Peters' own tendency is in the other direction. At several points in the article and especially in the conclusion he makes the cleavage between activity and passivity still deeper, and uses it to separate not just kinds of explanatory frameworks but kinds of dispositions as well; the term "motive" identifies the voluntary, purposive behavior, while "emotion" pertains to a set of automatic dispositions.

The way in which Peters divides up a state of mind into opposite sets of dispositions is best illustrated by his treatment of the emotion or passive side of the divide:

> Typically these appraisals are connected with the functioning of our autonomic nervous systems about which we usually speak in a metaphorical way but in metaphors which are consonant with our passivity. We boil and fume with anger; we tremble and sweat with fear; we swell and glow with pride; we blush with shame and embarrassment; our eyes dilate with fear, sparkle with delight and moisten with sorrow. Often, of course, the motor system is involved but, when it is, the manifestations typically take on an involuntary character. Our knees knock with fear, our teeth chatter with fright and sometimes our limbs are paralysed.[54]

Later in his essay Peters speaks of the passivity model as explaining "characteristic errors and distortions of thought," "motor slips and break-downs," and "dreaming and hysteria."[55] The range of phenomena included in all these examples is vast, but the general picture is clear enough: the passivity model or framework explains the cases where we are "acted on," or at least not acting, and all behavior which is "involuntary."[56]

---

[54]*Ibid.*, p. 121.

[55]*Ibid.*, p. 133.

[56]This characterization of the passions as "breakdowns" of rational, voluntary, purposive activity seems to accord well with the passive manner of such behavior. But the tie between "passions" and "passivity" is not as close as the similarity of the words would lead one to suppose. Recently Irving Thalberg ("Verbs, Deeds, and What Happens to Us," *Theoria*, XXXIII [1967, Part 3], pp. 259-77) has challenged the assumption that activity and passivity are exhaustive categories for describing human behavior. Thalberg bases his analysis on the widely accepted view (shared by Peters in the article discussed above, "Emotions," pp. 117-18, on "causal" and "internal" relations) that *causal* relations are between events which may be conceived and described separately from each other, while *logical* ("conceptual" (cont...)

What sort of "appraisal"[57] of reality is this "emotional" appraisal supposed to be? Are we to treat all our fearful sweating, shuddering, and knee-knocking as appraisals of some hitherto unidentified variety? Apparently so; although, according to the "standard use" of "appraisals," to do so seems a ludicrous glorification of their lowly stature. The culmination of this line of reasoning comes at the end of the article, where he suggests[58] that the passivity framework is not "parasitic" on the activity framework but independent of it. He proposes that men launch empirical investigations to discover where the passivity framework applies, for example in the thinking of children.

It is hard to know what to make of this proposal. Is it indeed a conceptual description at all? Is it an empirical hypothesis? The questions can hardly be answered, since, because Peters has by this point lost interest in appealing to ordinary language, we do not know what kind of criteria he would wish to apply.

---

or "internal") relations are between events which are not thus separately conceivable (Thalberg, "Verbs," pp. 260-61). Now activity-passivity is an example of a logical relationship; one cannot conceive or describe "x being pushed by y" without implying that "y was pushed by x." But the cases which Peters uses as paradigms of passivity, the "breakdown" verbs (Thalberg uses the same expression for them, *ibid.*, p. 275), are just those which turn out to be the poorest candidates for the title of "logical" relations. "Breakdown" verbs are those in which the person has a lapse in control over his actions or a lapse of awareness (*ibid.*, pp. 272-75), such as stammering, staggering, fainting, and the like; but each of these events is describable by itself apart from its cause, and it is even perfectly conceivable that there may be no cause at all. They are therefore bound by causal and not logical relations, and accordingly they should not be taken as examples of activity-passivity.

Thalberg's arguments do not imply that emotions do not involve (and in extreme cases strongly involve) lapse of control over our actions. But he does show that in ordinary language, having a lapse of control is not being passive--these are different kinds of categories--and thus that by Peters' own standard there is no direct bond between the passions Peters describes and passivity.

[57] Peters, "Emotions," p. 121, "implied appraisals"; according to *ibid.*, pp. 127-28, these appraisals are independent of a grasp of reality, since they are part of a "magical" view of the world.

[58] *Ibid.*, pp. 133-34.

D. The Conflict of Passion and Reason

Peters and Spinoza: Despite the ambiguities in his article, or perhaps partly because of them, Peters represents in his argumentation a view common in both philosophical and non-philosophical circles, which holds that the passions are the enemies of intellectual activity. The great champion of this standpoint in the history of thought is Spinoza, who dedicated all his energies to the ideal of the dispassionate life. But the viewpoint is not confined to him. Many others express similar notions, though few manage to achieve his congruence between thought and life.

Indeed, there are many aspects of Peters' article which recall Spinoza's description of the passions. What is needed to make Peters' program a great deal like that of Spinoza is an amendment of Peters' article in the direction of making more allowance for differences of degree between activity and passivity; and although Peters prefers to talk of a sharp break between "motives" and "emotions," there seems no reason why he would have to reject such a change. The Spinoza-Peters scheme would look like this:

(1) There is first of all a scale of mental states from complete "passivity" (states such as sleep, hysteria, and the like) to the completely active making of rational judgments.

(2) Parallel to this is a range of characterizations of these states going from "involuntary" to "voluntary," which recalls Spinoza's movement from "bondage" to "human freedom."

(3) Coordinate with these changes comes also a variation in the nature of the "appraisal" of the situation involved, running from vague for the passive states to clear for the active states.

(4) Likewise there is a radical difference in the value of the appraisals made: the passive appraisal is a "pretty poor sort of judgment"[59] and it is only the active which appraises with

---

[59]*Ibid.*, p. 120.

"the grasp of means and ends which conform to standards of efficiency and social appropriateness."[60]

This is not to say that there are not differences between the argument structures of Spinoza and Peters. Whereas Spinoza begins in his analysis from the clarity and distinctness of judgments Peters takes as his starting point the activity/passivity distinction, but the results are largely the same. Moreover, Peters has nothing to say about the third factor, suffering and joy, which Spinoza coordinates with the other two pairs; but it is perhaps not stretching Peters' article very much to say that this aspect, too, is implied in a scale which moves from breakdown and hysteria to freedom and rational judgment.

The Distrust of the Passions: There is something very natural and persuasive about this scale in which clarity, freedom, and dispassion wax and wane together. If one is to create an overall theory of the passions which will set up the logical coordinates of a map of which each individual passion is a segment—a project to fascinate any speculative philosopher—then here may be a good place to begin.

Nor is this set of correlations of interest only to the theorist of the passions. Although it does suggest the elementary structure from which Spinoza and Peters build up their far more intricate and subtle analyses, it represents also a number of popular and unformalized notions which often go unchallenged. The ideas cohere with a certain grass-roots distrust of emotionalism in the intellectual life, and with some persistent, commonplace versions of the geometric ideal of knowledge.

But to discuss the wholesale distrust of the passions is not an easy thing. Spinoza's treatment *more geometrico* is so abstract that it is hard to see where it begins. From where do the axioms and definitions derive with which he operates so freely? On the other hand, popular conceptions are too undefined to provide a firm basis for discussion. Peters' article gives a useful middle ground between formalism and chaos, and thus may be used as a representative spokesman for the general concern over the danger of emotions disrupting intellectual activity.

---

[60] *Ibid.*, p. 133.

The starting point for Peters' argument, it will be recalled, is a number of instances from the standard usage of the term "emotion" where it suggests a "pretty poor sort of judgment."[61] "Emotions," he writes, "like the weather, come over us and one of their main functions is to distort and cloud judgment."[62] And it is this function of the term which Peters uses to provide the clue to the "distinctive" feature[63] of the concept of emotion.

Peters' analogy between emotions and the weather is a suggestive one in ways which he perhaps did not anticipate. As with "emotion," we are more likely to employ the term "weather" when the climate is changeable or extreme or at least unusual. To single out a person or a judgment or a situation as "emotional" is to mark it as overly charged with emotion, usually of an unpleasant sort. Similarly, to speak of "having had a great deal of weather lately" indicates that one has just passed through an unsettled and stormy session. So also with some of the derivatives from "weather": the seas which the ship "weathers" are tempest-tossed, and the dingy water-side shack has been "weather-beaten" or "weathered" more by storms or baking sun than by the calms.

Thus far all is well with the argument both for emotions and the weather. The difficulty arises when Peters takes the cases of the stormy emotions as the "standard" use of the term "emotion," and leaves other functions out. It is as if one were to respond to "We had a great deal of weather lately" with the question, "Well, what were you having before that? How did you fill in the time when you weren't having weather?" The point is that the term "weather," like "emotion," operates both in a very broad way to bring together calm and stormy situations alike, and also in a narrower sense to pick out the most remarkable and especially the most disagreeable cases in the general category. It is a mistake to take the narrower sense as the "distinctive" sense of the term. The standard cases of emotion are not just those in which it warps or distorts, though these are common enough, any

---

[61] *Ibid.*, p. 120.

[62] *Ibid.*, pp. 119-20.

[63] *Ibid.*, p. 119.

more than the standard cases of weather (anywhere, perhaps, but in England) are the squalls and dingy fogs.

One may well be doubtful that this highly variegated batch of affairs called emotions has any function in common at all, but if there is such a central function it is not distortion.[64] Take, for a set of examples, hope, joy, and love. We may say that a man gave his life and did it "with hope in his heart," "with joy on his lips," "in loving devotion to his country." All of these constructions are presumably of the emotion sort according to Peters, since the prepositions make them stress the manner rather than the motive of his action. Yet it would surely be premature, once we know only that the patriot made an "emotional" judgment in this sense, to say that this was a "pretty poor judgment," or that he made a "pretty good judgment" either, for that matter. Emotions were involved, but unless they were extreme or out of place they need not have distorted his judgment. It may well have been that if he had judged *without* feeling any emotion his judgments would have been warped.

This last point creates particular difficulties for any account of the passions according to which the clearer the situation is kept in mind, the fewer passions one has, and the better one's judgments are. A common example used by theorists of the passions is courage/fear: when a person is beset by fear he is unable to assess his predicament clearly, but when he thinks dispassionately courage replaces his fear. Without in any way dismissing this example, one may question that it is enough to show the general correlation postulated. There are surely instances where the fit is not at all neat. Take the familiar parody of Kipling's lines:

> If you can keep your head when all about you
> Are losing theirs and blaming it on you --
> Maybe you don't fully appreciate the gravity of the
>   situation!

Sometimes having a clear view of the facts is exhibited in having fearful qualms and the urge to flee. Failure to experience these is a sign not of courage but of foolhardiness.

The same sort of observation could, of course, be made about the emotion of love. What seems to be the case in all of

---

[64] Cf. C. A. Mace, "Emotions and the Category of Passivity," *PAS* (1961-62), pp. 135-38.

the concrete examples of emotion which we bring up--with the exception of those Peters chooses for his paradigms, in which the emotion creates a total breakdown of the agent's control over his awareness and his actions--is that activity and passivity, clarity and unclarity, and the rest must all be inextricably mixed up together in an emotion for it to have its special character. Rationality does not inhere in any one aspect of the emotion situation but in the situation as a whole.

Of course nothing which has been said here counts against the evident fact that there are frequent occasions when passions do get in the way of the efficient execution of some rational activities. One cannot solve complex geometrical problems if one's mind keeps turning to his lady love, and one will not be able to form a balanced and scholarly assessment of the world's economic ills if one cowers in constant terror at the threat of imminent personal annihilation. But these cases are not *the* standard cases of emotion. Perhaps there are no paradigms which hold for the whole panoply of emotional behavior. Over against such paradigms it is necessary to be reminded that when the above man leaves his geometry and thinks about his lady love, he will need to be involved in the passion of love if he is to make the appropriate judgments in the situation. Again, if the second man is to face his personal danger courageously, he must at the same time feel fear but carry on despite his fear. It is easier to see this point in the cases where passion terms evaluate a situation positively--such as love, hope, or awe--than in cases of anger or fear. Perhaps this is one reason why the latter emotions are the favorite examples for philosophical discussion of those who sympathize with the view of Spinoza and Peters. But the point holds nevertheless: for certain cases (and important ones at that) the possession and even the conscious development of the appropriate passions is the indispensable prerequisite for making the correct assessment and behaving in the proper fashion. In a sense, then, the traditional warfare between passion and reason, hymned in so many philosophical treatises of the rationalistic period, is suspended in these cases, since instead of becoming caught up in strife passion and reason find themselves here inseparable allies. But their alliance will endure only as long as reason is not restricted too closely to the geometric ideal.

This helps to explain also why it proves so misleading to lump the emotions under the heading of "passivity." For "being passive" in the way the expression has been taken by some philosophers tends to mean that passions just happen to a person and that, accordingly, human intelligence and responsibility "break down" and have no essential role to play in the passions as such. But we are responsible for what we do when we love, fear, hope, and feel awe, and the utmost in concentration of human intelligence and moral endeavor is required. That the emotions should be at the same time both "passions" and "actions" in this way will be puzzling to anyone who operates with a sharp division between the active and the passive or between "motives" and "emotions"; but when one fastens his attention on the concrete cases involved the paradox vanishes and the mixture of active and passive in these situations becomes the most natural thing imaginable.

E. Conclusions

Philosophical Views on the Passions: The approaches which have been discussed within this chapter may be divided in two ways: first, into the "regularity" (Hume and Ryle) and "rationality" (Spinoza, Bedford, and Peters) viewpoints; and secondly, into those which do not rest their cases upon an explicit appeal to ordinary language (Spinoza and Hume) and those which do (Ryle, Bedford, and Peters).

(1) At least with respect to the question of the justification of the passions, Spinoza, Bedford, and Peters put forward a far more plausible account than the "regularity" view. Hume's very limited allowance for the justification of passions and Ryle's attempts to analyze motives into kinds of dispositions both attempt to reduce the evaluational aspect of emotions in order to meet the requirements of one model or another drawn indirectly from natural science. Their theories get what force they possess from the relative neatness with which they cohere with certain views of physical science, as compared with the potential confusion which is introduced when one tries to allow fully and fairly for both causal and teleological explanation. But as soon as the notions about motives, goals, purposes, and the like in everyday life and languages are taken seriously, the analyses of Hume and Ryle are seen to overlook the ordinary distinctions. This situation might not bother Hume, who is not

averse to going against commonsensical ideas when they conflict with the implications of Lockean psychology; but it should disturb Ryle, who claims to begin and end with ordinary language.

The type of view on the passions which has been called here the "rationalistic" approach, on the other hand, is especially adapted to deal with the distinction between teleological and causal explanation. The opposition within Spinoza's writings between reason and passion and in Bedford's between "motive" and "emotion" is evidence of this concern.

(2) Involved with the issue of justifying emotions is the methodological question which has been raised concerning the appeal to ordinary language.

The latter question is not a simple one. For in the broad sense in which the ordinary language theorists speak of "language"--including within the term the characteristic ways of human action as well as speaking--Spinoza and Hume make such an appeal too, though not with the explicitness of the later philosophers. The "human nature" with which these traditional philosophers deal is not far removed from that exhibited by the users of ordinary language.

Moreover, in none of the cases have the ordinary language philosophers altogether achieved a complete picture. Ryle's classification of motives as kinds of propensities overlooks teleological features of common discourse which cannot be simply dismissed. Bedford leaves out those aspects of emotions in which we are said to "feel" them. Peters makes a sharp division between feelings and motives and between passivity and activity which will not apply in many undoubted cases of emotional behavior.

But these problems do not indicate that there is something wrong with the appeal to ordinary language. On the contrary, the corrective which needs to be used in each case is not some standard above or beyond ordinary language, but rather a closer inspection of more and more cases of common paradigms of speech and action. The procedure these men follow is not mistaken but may not have been carried far enough.

The Passion of Faith: The result of looking at the treatments of passion discussed in this chapter is to expand one's awareness of the richness and ambiguity of the concept of passion. The traditional dichotomy of passion and reason brands the passions as passive and irrational because they do not fit the geometric ideal. Some contemporary philosophy has tended to perpetuate that narrow conception of passion, by treating the emotions as behavioral regularities or else as breakdowns of rational functioning; but although each of these present-day views has support in ordinary language, they conflict with each other, suggesting that the concept of passion is more varied than can be accounted for by either approach. Moreover, both the traditional and the contemporary discussions usually begin from a small set of stock examples (typically, fear and anger), and even a brief glance at the wealth of instances of human emotions brings up examples which strain the philosophical paradigms.

The purpose of this chapter, however, has not been to provide material for a general theory of the passions, but to clear the way for an examination of some distinctive features of the passion of faith. Once the spell cast by the vision of a warfare between passion and reason is lifted, a whole new set of questions can be asked about the passions, and the list of passions itself grows more varied, to include love, joy, hope, and awe; and it is to this latter group of passions that the passion of faith belongs.

CHAPTER TWO

CLIMACUS: "FAITH IS A HAPPY PASSION"

A. Theses Attributable to Johannes Climacus

Faith and the Passions: Near the end of the previous chapter[1] a number of cases of passions were suggested for which the classical dichotomy of passion versus reason does not adequately allow. At least with regard to these passions, of which the passion of love is the most obvious example, it does not hold that in virtue of the fact that they are passions they are unclear, unreasonable, or in any usual sense conducive to passivity. Moreover, the attempt to remedy the situation by carving up these passions into the part which is passionate and the part which is a motive, emotion, or something else, is not a step in the right direction. The fault lies in postulating the deep cleft between passion and reason in the first place.

The passion of faith, if it is a passion at all, must surely be grouped along with the cases just cited. If it is a passion ... for in some respects it is an anomaly even in the highly diversified collection which goes under that title. Although most, if not all, of the passions include some sort of awareness of a state of affairs, faith is a special case, in that the concepts of knowing and believing are more closely involved than in the other passions. There are, for instance, articles of faith; but are there in any similar sense "articles" of love, anger, or fear? Perhaps one might speak of "articles" of hope--hope that x is the case--but even here the expression is strained.

Kierkegaard in the *Fragments* and the *Postscript* speaks of this feature of the passion of faith in terms of a "how" and a "what," that is, "how" the person holds the faith and "what" is believed. Kierkegaard argues that all too frequently in intellectual and ecclesiastical circles the articles (the "what") of faith are seized upon as the all-important factor; and as a result the "how," the way in which the "what" is subjectively maintained, is overlooked. A better picture of faith can be achieved, he holds, by taking one's lead from the "how" of faith

---

[1]*Supra*, Chapter One, Section D, pp. 31-36.

rather than from the "what." Kierkegaard's statement in the
Climacean writings that "Faith is a happy passion" is his way of
emphasizing in the strongest possible way the overlooked "how"
of faith--those features which it shares with certain of the passions, and particularly the passion of love.

This chapter shall examine the passages in Kierkegaard's
writings which discuss faith as a passion and the distinction
between the "how" and the "what" of faith, in order to learn
some of the ways in which he relates the concepts of knowing,
believing, and feeling with respect to the Christian faith.

Five Theses: In order to fasten attention quickly upon
the parts of Kierkegaard's discussion of the concepts of faith
and passion in the Climacean writings and to be able to refer to
the parts easily, we shall begin with a group of "theses"[2] drawn
mainly from the *Fragments* and the *Postscript*:

(1) Faith is a happy passion.[3]
(2) Subjectivity is truth.[4]
(3) Subjectivity is untruth.[5]
(4) The paradox and the passion are a mutual fit.[6]

---

[2] The term "theses" here has a somewhat special sense. It derives from a chapter in the *Postscript* entitled "Theses Possibly or Actually Attributable to Lessing," in which Climacus praises Lessing as a Socratic figure who does not pose as an authority but only reminds his readers of what they already know. Similarly, in what follows it would be quite contrary to the spirit in which Climacus offers his "theses" to suppose that he puts them up for philosophical debate.

[3] *Fragments*, pp. 76, 105; *Postscript*, p. 51. The expression is characteristic of the Climacus authorship but not altogether restricted to it. See, for example, *Fear and Trembling* (Garden City, N. Y., 1954), p. 77: "Faith is a miracle, and yet no man is excluded from it; for that in which all human life is unified is passion, and faith is a passion."

[4] This thesis and the following one are formulated in a number of ways in the *Postscript* within the chapter entitled "The Subjective Truth, Inwardness; Truth is Subjectivity," pp. 169-224. For the notion that "Subjectivity is truth" or "Subjectivity is the truth," see esp. pp. 181-84, 248, and *passim*.

[5] *Ibid.*, pp. 185ff.

[6] *Ibid.*, p. 206.

Theses 41

(5) If the "how" is truly given, then the "what" is also given.[7]

In this formidable assembly of statements we find sketched not only some important features of faith and passion but also a number of the leading ideas which inform the Climacean corpus.

The first thesis represents also the thesis of this chapter. The sense in which faith is a "happy" passion, however, is a matter which will be left for later discussion.[8]

The second and third theses are two of the best known and least understood sentences that Kierkegaard ever wrote. The theses point up a distinction between general religiosity, which is available to every man through a development of the religious

---

[7] The source for this quotation is an entry in Søren Kierkegaard's diary for the year 1849: "In all that is usually said about Johannes Climacus being purely subjective and so on, people have forgotten, in addition to everything else concrete about him, that in one of the last sections he shows that the curious thing is: that there is a 'how' which has this quality, that if *it* is truly given, then the 'what' is also given; and that it is the 'how' of 'faith'. Here, quite certainly, we have inwardness at its maximum proving to be objectivity once again. And this is an aspect of the principle of subjectivity which, so far as I know, has never before been presented or worked out." X^2 A 299 (Dru 1021). The reference is presumably to the conclusion of the *Postscript*, esp. pp. 537-44, where the following statements appear:

"The pathos of appropriation needs to be so defined that it cannot be confused with any other pathos" (p. 538).

"SUBJECTIVELY, WHAT IT IS TO BECOME A CHRISTIAN IS DEFINED THUS: The decision lies in the subject. The appropriation is the paradoxical inwardness which is specifically different from all other inwardness. The thing of being a Christian is not determined by the *what* of Christianity but by the *how* of the Christian. This *how* can only correspond with one thing, the absolute paradox.... Faith is the objective uncertainty due to the repulsion of the absurd held fast by the passion of inwardness, which in this instance is intensified to the utmost degree. This formula fits only the believer, no one else, not a lover, not an enthusiast, not a thinker, but simply and solely the believer who is related to the absolute paradox (p. 540).

" ... the 'how' of the individual is an expression just as precise and more decisive for what he has, than is the 'what' to which he appeals ... " (p. 541).

" ... a man merely by describing the 'how' of his inwardness can show indirectly that he is a Christian without mentioning God's name" (p. 542).

[8] See the section on "offense" in this chapter, *infra*, pp. 60-61, Section D, 2, b; and also the conclusion of Chapter Four, with regard to the passionate rejection of faith, pp. 113-116.

elements of his subjectivity, and the Christian faith, which can only be appropriated when the subjectivity of a man has been transformed by the historical Incarnation.

"Subjectivity is truth," although it seems to represent the ultimate in irrationality, comes in fact of an ancient and honorable philosophical lineage. It is Climacus' version (via Lessing, as he notes[9]) of the Socratic view that with respect to ethical and certain other sorts of knowledge one cannot learn anything really new, since one already has this knowledge (in his "subjectivity," one might say) and needs only to be reminded of it.[10] Socrates knows that there are kinds of knowledge which are "objective" in that they simply cannot be recollected (the precise date of his own death, for example)[11] but these are not the sorts of knowledge which occupy his primary attention. That kind which does concern him, above all that about ethical and religious matters, he does not think can be taught, because it resides within every man. All that can be done is to goad the pupil to "know" explicitly and effectively that which he has in another sense "known" all along. And since to know about ethical matters in the effective sense is to be able to act ethically, Socrates can say in his gnomic way, "Virtue is knowledge."

"Subjectivity is untruth," on the other hand, rejects the avenue of recollection, but does not go back to the notion which

---

[9] *Postscript*, pp. 67-113, esp. p. 71.

[10] The *Fragments* (pp. 11-16) cites for its interpretation of Socrates a number of dialogues, especially *Meno* 80 with its "pugnacious proposition" about knowledge. Thulstrup in his commentary on the *Fragments* (*ibid.*, pp. 172-73) expands on Climacus' references and shows the various ways in which the doctrine is developed in Plato. Climacus' later work, the *Postscript*, p. 184n, corrects the presentation within the *Fragments* and distinguishes between Socrates and Plato.

Kierkegaard's picture of Socrates is indebted to Hegel, for example to Hegel's *Lectures on the History of Philosophy* (New York, 1955), I, p. 410, II, pp. 32-34. Kierkegaard's dissertation, entitled *The Concept of Irony: With Constant Reference to Socrates* (New York, 1965), adapts for its own purposes a number of Hegelian notions, such as the inner/outer and subjective/objective dichotomies, and also makes a typological differentiation between Socrates and Christ. (See introduction to the *Concept of Irony* by Lee Capel, pp. 30-37, and text, pp. 52 note and 242 note.)

[11] Certainly Climacus makes such a distinction, e.g., in the *Postscript*, pp. 176-77.

Socrates rejected, that objectivity is truth. Instead, Kierkegaard's Climacus "goes beyond Socrates" in the only way he can see open, accepting the negative thesis that ethical and religious knowledge cannot be learned from another person, but setting up also a different and more stringent negative thesis, that with respect to a limited but existentially crucial area of knowledge one cannot learn from oneself either. For this particular ethico-religious subject matter (that which Climacus calls the "Absolute Paradox" or Incarnation) the Socratic option is closed and hence "Subjectivity is untruth." If there is to be any knowledge in such an area, it can only arise within the context of a new subjectivity (a new passion, a new inwardness, a new "how") to which recollection gives no access.

The fourth and fifth theses do not parallel the distinction made by the previous two. The "mutual fit" is between the distinctively Christian passion and the Incarnation, and the "how" and the "what" are also both specifically Christian. These two theses, therefore, belong to that side of the divide on which "Subjectivity is untruth."

Although the fourth and fifth theses are applied by the *Postscript* to Christianity (where subjectivity is untruth), however, they fit even more easily with the type of religiosity associated with the thesis that subjectivity is truth. Accordingly, the procedure adopted here will be to introduce these two theses first in the context of general religiosity, and then as they describe Christian faith. Such an approach is implicit in Kierkegaard's own presentation in the *Postscript*, where the notion of subjectivity is explained initially with respect to general religiosity, and only later applied to the specifically Christian situation.

B. The "How" and the "What"

Direct and Indirect Communication: Before developing the contrast between "Subjectivity is truth" and "Subjectivity is untruth," we shall find it helpful to look again at what Kierkegaard means by the "how"[12] and by "Socratic knowledge."

---

[12] This approach to Kierkegaard via the "how"/"what" distinction is indebted to a number of articles by Paul L. Holmer, especially "Kierkegaard as a Critic," *Religion on Campus*, I (Spring, 1965), pp. 4-7, 10; and also to Carl Michalson, "Kierkegaard's Theology of Faith," *Religion in Life*, XXXII (Spring, 1963), pp. 225-37.

In a set of lectures from 1847 which Kierkegaard several times revised but never completed or published,[13] a view is developed that there are two kinds of communication, one which provides information (a "what") and the other which provides a capability (a "how").

These pages represent an attempt by Kierkegaard to explain the kind of knowledge which the *Fragments* speaks of as "Socratic." The *Fragments* describes such knowledge as something present in every man and denies that the knowledge can be taught, since the teacher cannot give to the pupil that which the pupil already has. But what can this sort of knowledge be? Mystic intuitions? Innate ideas? Beyond referring the matter to Socrates, Climacus in the *Fragments* leaves the reader to his own devices.

In the lectures on communication Kierkegaard helps to guard against some possible misunderstandings, by means of a distinction between the communication of *information*, which has an "object" about which one learns, and the communication of *capability*, which does not. The former is given by science, and sometimes by rote-learning; but the latter, "Socratic" kind of communication is acquired by art, that is to say, by drill and training.[14] It is only with respect to the communication of capability that Socrates' "pugnacious proposition" of the *Meno* holds good, that one can learn nothing new. The reason that the proposition holds in that case is that, since this knowledge is the development of capacities we possess, it cannot provide us with anything which we do not already potentially have.[15]

---

[13] VIII^2 B 79, 81, 85-89 (all from 1847); trans. Hong (*Journals and Papers*, I, pp. 267-307).

[14] VIII^2 B 81:5 (Hong, I, pp. 268-69); VIII^2 B 83 (Hong, I, pp. 281-83); VIII^2 B 89, "Second Lecture" (Hong, I, pp. 303-08). The distinction is expressed in the Danish terms "kunnen" and "viden," which are cognate to the familiar German verbs "können" and "wissen."

[15] "In regard to the ethical and the ethical-religious, the genuine communication and instruction is *training* or *upbringing*. By upbringing a person becomes that which he is essentially regarded to be (a horse, if it is trained and the trainer has good sense, becomes precisely a horse). Upbringing begins with regarding the one who is going to be brought up as being κατὰ δύναμιν that which he shall become, and by regarding him from this point of view brings it out of him." VIII^2 B 82:12 (Hong, I, p. 279).

Kierkegaard finds the paradigm case of communication of capability in the example of ethical knowledge. Aesthetic capability he calls "indirect communication as a border region of direct communication."[16] And ethico-religious knowledge he fits under this heading only with certain reservations which we shall note later.[17]

But Kierkegaard is deeply uneasy about the approach he is taking to the distinction between direct and indirect communication. In an entry in his notebook about this time he decides that "The fact of the matter is that there ought not to be teaching; what I have to say may not be taught; by being taught it turns into something entirely different."[18] And even in the lectures he writes that he proceeds "not without many doubts and much hesitation,"[19] and he wonders out loud "whether this, the fact that now from a podium I begin to lecture about what I intend to lecture about, is not contradictory to what I am to lecture about."[20]

The "Climacus" Writings: In the *Fragments* and the *Postscript* Kierkegaard does not have to experience the same disquietudes, since he is not teaching about indirect communication but putting it into practice. He employs the distinction between the "how" and the "what" for a very particular purpose, to expose the incongruity which often exists between *what* a man says and *how* he says it and acts upon it. His tool here is that favorite weapon of Socrates--irony.

One of the most telling instances of the effectiveness of this irony comes when Kierkegaard's Climacus, in arguing against the popular view that the possession of the proper "what" is all-important, points out that the acceptance of correct opinions is not even sufficient to mark out a man as sane rather than mad.

---

[16]VIII^2 B 85:6-7 (Hong, I, pp. 284-85). But note that he has a broad view of the "aesthetic," and includes within it military exercises and dancing.

[17]Cf. *infra* in this chapter, footnote 37.

[18]VIII^1 A 554 n.d. 1848 (Hong, I, p. 265).

[19]VIII^2 B 88, "First Lecture" (Hong, I, p. 296).

[20]*Ibid.* (Hong, I, p. 297).

Climacus tells the story[21] of an inmate escaped from an asylum, who in order to avoid detection hits on the plan of frequently uttering an opinion with impeccable credentials. So, picking up a ball he finds lying by the road, he puts it in his back pocket, and each time as he takes a step and the ball strikes his rear, he calls out "Bang, the earth is round!" Since he does this, he thinks, all his friends will know that he is sane! The madman's mistake, however, does not consist in his having a wrong "what," and he will not be cured if a psychiatrist gets him to give up his widely respected truth and to believe instead that the world is flat as a pancake. The content which the escaped inmate offers as proof of his sanity is perfectly sound; but this "what" is rendered ridiculous by the "how" in which he presents it.

Although Climacus offers many examples of this sort of ironical incongruity, it is not until he comes to the instances in the religious sphere that the argument achieves full force. Here again there is a "what" which (by the state church of Denmark at least) can be taken for granted. Many would say that the "how" is so obvious that only the madman could mistake it. Others, more skeptical, question the respectability of the "what," and recommend suspension of belief until further study has been made. Climacus' position differs from both of these: the problem, he says, is in the "how," and the task of the religious writer should be to show how extremely difficult, in fact almost impossible, it is to realize the "how" in everyday life.

To make his point Climacus conducts a "thought-experiment" through many pages in the *Postscript*,[22] in which he examines the "how" for the text "A man can do nothing of himself, but with God he can do everything." The parson delivers this message in his sermon on Sunday, and he speaks so eloquently that all the people nod their heads in agreement and some even take notes on "what" is said. But that was on Sunday; and on Monday Climacus sends a spy out to Deer Park (Copenhagen's city park) to find the parishioners and discover how well they actually understand the principle that a man can do nothing of himself. Monday the spy finds parishioners. Tuesday, Wednesday, and Thursday he finds more. But the principle that by themselves they can do nothing (which

---

[21]*Postscript*, p. 174.

[22]*Ibid.*, pp. 417 to about 449.

they understood very well on Sunday) does not stop any of them from taking a stroll (of themselves) through Deer Park, or from doing (of themselves) any number of other things. And as for the rest of the sermon, that with God they can do everything, why, it is hard to imagine what they are to do with this notion in the concrete cases.

Nor is the parishioners' difficulty simply a matter of finding themselves in a particularly stringent life-setting with an especially stern text. Deer Park does not threaten them with martyrdom, nor is this text more puzzling than many others which the pastor expounds at length on Sunday, and which they understand very well, they say. Yet the strange thing is that on weekdays it is not the momentous actions which are hard to do "with God," but that the more insignificant an action is, the more difficult it is to perform in this way![23] The whole human calculus is turned upside-down, and with it also is abolished the differential among human beings--wise and foolish, strong and weak, learned and untaught--with respect to ability to perform tasks. In the abstract the preacher's sermon seemed simple; but when the principle is brought into connection with particular moments, moods, states of mind, and circumstances, then the overwhelming difficulty of the "how" is exposed.

What Climacus suggests by his Deer Park experiment is not that religious truth is easy to understand but difficult to apply. The easy understanding which the parishioners had on Sunday is only of a trivial sort, and in any religiously important sense they cannot be said to grasp the sermon unless they have a command over the "how" which goes with it. The observations of the spy go to show that, whatever claims to understanding they might put forward, the parishioners did not know what was being talked about when the parson said "Of yourself you can do nothing, but with God you can do everything." To have the "what" they had to have the "how" which went with it, for the "how" is the formal condition for the "what."

C. The Mutual Fit of the "How" and the "What"

The fact that having the "how" is in some way the condition for having the "what" presupposes two things: first, that

---

[23]*Ibid.*, pp. 435ff.

there are kinds of subjectivity, passion, inwardness--that is, kinds of "how"--to go with the varieties of content;[24] and second, that there is a certain "fit" between a "how" and its "what."

The latter proposition is an extremely important one which deserves careful attention. Climacus gives us, in fact, two very different ways in which the "how" may fit the "what."[25] Although neither Climacus nor his commentators are always scrupulous in distinguishing these two ways, the difference between them is utterly essential, since it is based on the cleft between general religiosity and Christianity (what Climacus calls "Religiousness A" and "Religiousness B"), and between "Subjectivity is truth" and "Subjectivity is untruth." Let us examine these two sides in turn.

1. If Subjectivity is Truth ...

Although the way in which Climacus explains the relationship between "how" and "what" in the Socratic scheme may appear frighteningly abstruse, the matter is basically quite simple. In an early part of the *Postscript* he writes:

> In every case where the object of knowledge is the very inwardness of the subjectivity of the individual, it is necessary for the knower to be in a corresponding condition.[26]

What is the "object of knowledge" here? Climacus speaks of it as the "very inwardness of the subjectivity of the individual," a formulation which leaves us almost as much in the dark as before.

---

[24] Climacus speaks of "Christianity, which is precisely inwardness, though not any and every type of inwardness" (*ibid.*, p. 251), and he insists that "it is possible to exist with inwardness also outside Christianity" (*ibid.*, p. 248). Cf. the remark in Kierkegaard's papers from 1844: "Let no one misunderstand all my talk about passion and pathos to mean that I am proclaiming any and every uncircumcised immediacy, all manner of unshaven passion." V A 44 (Dru 488).

[25] In what follows the fourth and fifth theses are applied to both Religiousness A and to Religiousness B. As was noted earlier, however, the context for both of these theses indicates that Climacus is making them about Christianity. The reason for applying them to Religiousness A as well is that they apply more obviously to A than to B, so that it is easier to see their application to A than in the contexts where the theses are in fact introduced.

[26] *Postscript*, p. 51.

More light on the topic comes from the discussion in the *Postscript* immediately following the famous passage which states that he who prays to a false God in a true spirit prays to the true God, whereas he who prays to the true God falsely prays to an idol.[27] At this point Climacus brings forward his crucial distinction between the "how" and the "what," between subjectivity and objectivity.

> *The objective accent falls on WHAT is said, the subjective accent on HOW it is said.* This distinction holds even in the aesthetic realm, and receives definite expression in the principle that what is in itself true may in the mouth of such and such a person become untrue.... Aesthetically the contradiction that truth becomes untruth in this or that person's mouth, is best construed comically: In the ethico-religious sphere, accent is again on the "how." But this is not to be understood as referring to demeanor, expression, or the like; rather it refers to the relationship sustained by the existing individual, in his own existence, to the content of his utterance. Objectively the interest is focussed merely on the thought-content, subjectively on the inwardness. At its maximum this inward "how" is the passion of the infinite, and the passion of the infinite is the truth. But the passion of the infinite is precisely subjectivity, and thus subjectivity becomes the truth.[28]

Then he proceeds to state the relationship between the "how" and the "what":

> Objectively there is no infinite decisiveness, and hence it is objectively in order to annul the difference between good and evil, together with the principle of contradiction, and therewith also the infinite difference between the true and the false. Only in subjectivity is there decisiveness, to seek objectivity is to be in error. It is the passion of the infinite that is the decisive factor and not its content, *for its content is precisely itself*. In this manner subjectivity and the subjective "how" constitute the truth.[29]

"Its content is precisely itself" he says; then of course passion and paradox correspond to each other, since they are made for each other, conceptually intertwined from the beginning.

---

[27] *Ibid.*, pp. 178-80.

[28] *Ibid.*, p. 181. Italics in original.

[29] *Ibid.* Italics mine.

For if the manner of appropriation *is* the content then one should not be surprised if they both fit each other.

This way of formulating the matter, however, may be puzzling. For if one identifies the "how" and the "what" by saying of the "how" that "Its content is precisely itself" then the two become indistinguishable and the assertion of their identity seems to lose its point. A more complete statement of the relationship comes later in the *Postscript*, when Climacus speaks of the "what" of religion as being the highest human *telos*, eternal happiness, which must be willed for its own sake.[30] And one would not speak of the "how" as a *telos*, but rather as the way in which the *telos* is to be achieved. But as soon as one tries to go further in specifying the nature of this *telos* one gets a rude shock, because eternal happiness, Climacus insists again and again, is "*definable solely in terms of the mode of acquisition*," the "how."[31]

---

[30]*Ibid.*, p. 353.

[31]*Ibid.*, p. 382. Italics in original. The context for the statement is as follows: "And this is why an eternal happiness as the absolute good has the remarkable trait of *being definable solely in terms of the mode of acquisition*. Other goods, precisely because the mode of acquisition is accidental, or at any rate subject to a relative dialectic, must be defined in terms of the good itself. Money, for example, may be acquired both with and without effort on the part of the possessor, and both modes of acquisition are again subject to manifold variations; but money, nevertheless, remains the same good.... But there is nothing to be said of an eternal happiness except that it is the good which is attained by venturing everything absolutely. Every description of the glory of this good is already as it were an attempt to make several different modes of acquisition possible, one easier for example, and one more difficult. This is enough to prove that the description does not really describe the absolute good, but only imagines itself doing so, while essentially dealing with relative goods.... This is why discourse concerning this good may be so brief, for there is only one thing to say: venture everything! There are no anecdotes to tell how Peter became rich by hard work, and Paul by playing the lottery ... and so forth. But in another sense the discourse may be very long, the longest of all discourses, because really to venture everything requires a conscious clarity with respect to oneself which is acquired only slowly. Here is the task of the religious address. Were it merely to say the brief word: 'Venture everything', there would not be needed more than one speaker in an entire kingdom, while the longest discourse must not forget the venture. The religious address may deal with anything and everything, if only it constantly brings everything into relationship with the absolute category of religiosity." Cf. *ibid.*, p. 383.

True to his principle, Climacus goes on to define the religious "what" strictly in terms of the way it is acquired. What is eternal happiness? What is the highest goal for which men seek? Climacus devotes many pages to the question, but the only answers are given in terms of the religious "how," or "existential pathos."

> (1) As the "initial expression" of this pathos he gives us "infinite resignation": the motto of the religious person is "Venture everything!"[32]
>
> (2) Nor does the next chapter specify any more details about the bliss in store for those who seek eternal happiness; for the "essential expression" is suffering, and the religious orator who knows his calling will not tell his listeners that the suffering has a happy ending--instead he will proclaim only more and greater suffering![33]
>
> (3) The "decisive expression" is the most strenuous of all--that the person is "totally or essentially guilty"[34]--but what does this tell us of the nature of eternal happiness? Nothing, because eternal happiness can only be described indirectly; only the "how" can define the religious "what."

The reason that the religious *telos* cannot be specified is not an accidental one which can perhaps be remedied by further inquiry, but has to do with the nature of this "what" as the goal for ethical striving. "The resolved individual does not even wish to know anything more about this *telos* than that it exists, for as soon as he acquires some knowledge about it, he already begins to be retarded in his striving."[35] The only appropriate understanding lies not in "testifying about an eternal happiness,

---

[32] *Ibid.*, pp. 382-83.

[33] *Ibid.*, p. 395.

[34] *Ibid.*, p. 471; cf. p. 475.

[35] *Ibid.*, p. 353.

but in transforming one's existence into a testimony concerning it."[36]

We began with the first thesis, that faith is a passion, and from the second thesis, which states that subjectivity is truth. Now we find that on this hypothesis the content of faith and the faith itself are the same. How stands it then with the fifth thesis, that where the "how" is truly given, the "what" is also given? The answer is that since the "how" and the "what" have the same description, where the "how" is given, the "what" *must* be given. And so we arrive again at the Socratic position that in these matters we can learn nothing new; for if we know the "how" we know also the "what," and to be a man is to have the capacity-knowledge of the "how."

2. If Subjectivity is Untruth ...

The relationship between the "how" and the "what" in Christianity is quite different from that which has just been charted above for that general religiosity of a Kantian sort which Climacus labels "Religiousness A." Christianity essentially involves a content, the Incarnation. Indeed, this "what" is its alpha and omega. Because the Incarnation is an historical fact, although of an extremely unusual kind, it is in some senses identifiable independently from the specifically Christian "how," and can therefore be specified in ways which the "what" in Religiousness A could not.

The implications of this difference between Religiousness A and Religiousness B (Christianity) are:

(a) In Religiousness B the nature of eternal happiness is specified in certain ways, but not so as to turn back to speculation. Here one may

> posit conditions, of such a sort that they are not merely deeper dialectical apprehensions of inwardness, but are a definite something which defines more closely the eternal happiness (whereas in A the only closer definitions are the closer definitions of inward apprehension), not defining more closely the individual apprehension of it, but defining more closely the eternal happiness itself, though not as a task for thought, but paradoxically as a repellent to produce new pathos.[37]

---

[36]*Ibid.*

[37]*Ibid.*, p. 494. Cf. the passages in Kierkegaard's papers on the need for there to be some sort of "knowledge" communicated before one can become a Christian. (Cont...)

The last phrase of this quotation is important. Although eternal happiness is further defined, this change does not lead away from passion but to greater passion, not towards speculation but into concrete existence. Accordingly, the positing of conditions defining eternal happiness does not stifle ethical striving but presses it as far as possible.

(b) The term "repellent" in the phrase above points to a crucial aspect of Climacus' view, an aspect which has received great, perhaps too great, attention. The way in which the "what" in Religiousness B, the Incarnation, "repels" and incites the existing person to greater passion is by its absurdity. Climacus devotes the concluding chapter of the *Postscript* largely to this factor, and he keeps so unflinchingly to his position, that the content of the Christian faith is absurd, that his pages have become standard references for philosophers who wish to illustrate the irrationality of religion.

A glance at the phrases and statements which Climacus uses will show how Climacus' writing lends itself to such application: the Incarnation is "the absolute paradox" and "the essentially incomprehensible";[38] it involves a "contradiction";[39] the

---

"The difference between upbringing in the ethical and upbringing in the ethical-religious is simply this--that the ethical is the universally human itself, but religious (Christian) upbringing must first of all communicate a knowledge. Ethically man as such knows about the ethical, but man as such does not know about the religious in the Christian sense. Here there must be the communication of a little knowledge first of all-- but then the same relationship as in the ethical enters in. The instruction, the communication, must not be as of a knowledge, but upbringing, practicing, art-instruction.
"My service in using pseudonyms consists in having discovered, Christianly, the maieutic method...." (VIII^2 B 82, 13 [Hong, I, pp. 279-80]).
"Religious capability or religious
   oughtness-capability
"Here is an element of knowledge and to that extent an object. But it is only a first thing. The communication is still not essentially of knowledge but a communication of capability. That there is an element of knowledge is particularly true for Christianity; a knowledge about Christianity must certainly be communicated in advance. But it is only a preliminary." (VIII^2 B 85:29 [Hong, I, p. 289])

[38] *Ibid.*, p. 499.

[39] *Ibid.*, p. 510.

Christian has the task to "endure the crucifixion of the understanding";[40] he is "nailed to the paradox"[41] which "conflicts with all thinking"[42] and can only be believed "against the understanding."[43]

Of course this collage of expressions cannot pretend to give a balanced picture of Climacus' conclusions, much less of his argument. And it is by no means settled just what those conclusions are. Perhaps the most hotly debated topic in contemporary Climacean scholarship revolves around the question of whether Climacus is committed in these pages to maintaining the Incarnation is a logical contradiction—a conclusion which according to any formal logic whatever would mean that Christian faith could not be believed or even thought.[44] One may attempt to lead him into this dead end, or try to release him from the apparent conclusions, but by and large it is the former course which is the easier. For Climacus does not want to be rescued.

---

[40] *Ibid.*, p. 500.

[41] *Ibid.*, p. 512.

[42] *Ibid.*, Cf. p. 513 "breach with all thinking."

[43] *Ibid.*, pp. 504, 513.

[44] There is such a staggering quantity of secondary literature on the topics of the paradox, the absurd, and contradiction in Kierkegaard's authorship that even a bibliography of that literature would be massive.
    The position adopted here is one defended by Alastair McKinnon in "Kierkegaard: 'Paradox' and Irrationalism," *Journal of Existentialism*, XXVII (Spring, 1967), pp. 401-16. He writes: "When he [i.e., Kierkegaard] declares Christianity to be a paradox in this sense his point is really quite simple: it is that Christianity, or any other new view for that matter, *appears* to the would-be believer as a contradiction. Kierkegaard is not saying that Christianity actually is logically contradictory in and of itself. His point is simply that, as a new view, it necessarily conflicts with the would-be believer's earlier conceptions, and that one can *become* a believer only by first accepting a claim which, because of this conflict, is or at least appears to be logically self-contradictory. Many of Kierkegaard's iterations that Christianity must be accepted as a paradox are to be understood at least primarily in this way" (*ibid.*, pp. 408-09). Cf. McKinnon, "Barth's Relation to Kierkegaard: Some Further Light," *Canadian Journal of Theology*, XIII (January, 1967), pp. 31-41. An important part of the support for this view of Kierkegaard is derived from some texts out of Kierkegaard's later years which had previously not received much attention, and which have now been translated in Cornelio Fabro's "Faith and Reason in Kierkegaard's Dialectic," *A Kierkegaard Critique* (New York, 1962), pp. 156-206.

The Mutual Fit

He dreads the prospect of fitting the "what" of Christianity into a (suitably enlarged and remodeled) speculative edifice. This does not mean that he accepts the view that the Incarnation could only be believed by that gullible or feeble-minded minority who can swallow the notion of the existence of square circles and other logical absurdities. The difficulty is not in the "what"; the point of Climacus' talk about absurdity and the like is to place the problem where it truly is, in the "how." "Christianity as a thought-project is not difficult to understand," he writes; "the difficulty, the paradox, is that it is real."[45]

The reason the attempt to formulate the Incarnation in generally accessible scholarly categories fails and is bound to fail is not that this content is unintelligible, but that the approach of trying to understand this "what" by the way of erudition chooses the wrong "how." Once it is seen that the difficulty in understanding lies in using the proper "how," a person still has formidable obstacles to grasping it, but they are not the obstacles of accepting formal absurdities but rather of an extraordinarily demanding task of living Christianly. So difficult is the way of appropriating the Christian truth that Climacus himself makes little attempt even to describe it. He confines himself to portraying the far less demanding "how" of Religiousness A, which as we just saw is very difficult in its own right. The portrayal of the "how" of Religiousness B he leaves to others who are Christians (as he himself does not claim to be), and particularly to men such as Søren Kierkegaard in his later writings.[46]

(c) Although Religiousness B comes under the hypothesis of "Subjectivity is untruth," there is a sense in which it fits also under the rubric of "Subjectivity is truth."[47] The subjectivity which is truth in the case of Religiousness B, however, is a *new* subjectivity, the subjectivity of the "new creature" who has the passion of faith. This subjectivity, moreover, is not a universal capacity of men simply as men, but is a condition achieved through the transformation of the person through the power of the Incarnation.

---

[45]*Postscript*, p. 514.

[46]Cf. *supra*, Section D, 2 of this chapter on joy/suffering, pp. 61-62.

[47]*Postscript*, p. 206.

If the relationship between Religiousness A and Religiousness B is as has just been formulated, then the problem which was mentioned in the previous sub-section on the absurdity of the Christian "what" comes into perspective. For the logical absurdities which Climacus found when he tried to put the Incarnation into speculative categories are just the results one would expect if the categories of the Incarnation are different (because rooted in a different "how," or form of life) from those which speculative thought ascribes to men in general. Of course there will be "category mistakes" if one takes expressions which are appropriate to one form of life and fits them into schemes made for forms of life which conflict with it.

The test of this interpretation of Climacus would come if one could show that the categories in which the Incarnation are spoken of are as natural to the "how" of Religiousness B as the categories of Religiousness A are to its "how." But this is a statement Climacus cannot make because he has methodologically excluded himself from the position of being able to make it. He writes from Religiousness A[48] and using the categories of Religiousness A, so that he has no way of expressing the Incarnation without absurdity. But nothing which he says excludes the possibility that the "what" of Religiousness B is natural to its "how." And Kierkegaard wrote later, in response to a man who tried to make Climacus an irrationalist, that the formulations which seem absurd from the outside are the most natural thing possible for those who share the passion of faith.

> The Absurd is a category, it is the negative criterion for God or for the relationship to God. When the believer believes, the Absurd is not the Absurd--faith transforms it; but in every weak moment, to him it is again more or less the Absurd. The passion of faith is the only thing capable of mastering the Absurd. If this were not so, faith would not be faith in the strictest sense, but would be a kind of knowledge. The Absurd provides a negative demarcation of the sphere of faith, making it a sphere in itself. It must necessarily seem to a third party that the believer relates himself by virtue of the Absurd; for after all, the third party lacks the passion of faith.[49]

---

[48] More accurately, he writes from the position of a "humorist," between A and B.

[49] X^6 B 79 p. 85. (trans. Fabro, "Faith and Reason in Kierkegaard's Dialectic," *A Kierkegaard Critique* [New York, 1962], pp. 182-83). Cf. X^2 A 592 (Dru 1084) on "the absurd," and (cont...)

(d) But the difference between Religiousness A and Religiousness B cannot be simply that the latter has a new "how" or subjectivity. The way in which Religiousness B is defined implies that it will have a different relationship between the "how" and the "what" from that in Religiousness A. In Religiousness A one can say that the "how" is identical with the "what," at least in the sense that the only way to specify the "what" or *telos* is by describing the "how" of the person involved. But with Religiousness B, the "what" is the Incarnation, which is historical and not the specification of anyone's subjectivity. Accordingly, the conceptual tie in B between the "how" and the "what" must be of a looser sort than that in A.

What sort of linkage is there, then, between the "how" and the "what" in B? The quotation which was cited above says that Religiousness B includes the activity of "defining more closely the eternal happiness itself, though not as a task for thought, but paradoxically as a repellent to produce new pathos."[50] This suggests that one may arrive at a definition of the "what" which is not simply borrowed from an account of the "how," though the definition is for religious and not for speculative purposes. Climacus is guarding against the temptation either to derive the "what" from the "how"--to specify the propositional content of the belief by means of the dispositions and the like of the person believing[51]--or on the other hand to try to handle the "what" apart from the "how" in which it has its point. He maintains that there is a "mutual fit" between the "how" and the "what," but not a mutual entailment, and summarizes the relationship in the following way:

> Suppose ... that subjectivity is the truth, and that subjectivity is an existing subjectivity, then, if I may so express myself, Christianity fits perfectly into the picture. Subjectivity culminates in passion, Christianity is the paradox, paradox and passion are a mutual fit, and the paradox is altogether suited to one whose situation is, to be in the

---

especially the sentence: "While naturally it is a matter of course that for him who believes it [i.e., the content of faith] is not the absurd."

[50] *Postscript*, p. 494.

[51] As might be done, for example, with the content of Religiousness A.

> extremity of existence. Aye, never in all the
> world could there be found two lovers so wholly
> suited to one another as paradox and passion, and
> the strife between them is like the strife between
> lovers, when the dispute is about whether he first
> aroused her passion, or she his. And so it is
> here; the existing individual has by means of the
> paradox itself come to be placed in the extremity
> of existence. And what can be more splendid for
> lovers than that they are permitted a long time
> together without any alteration in the relation-
> ship between them, except that it becomes more
> intensive in inwardness? And this is indeed
> granted to the highly unspeculative understanding
> between passion and the paradox, since the whole
> of life in time is vouchsafed, and the change
> comes first in eternity.[52]

The metaphor is a masterful one: the "how" and the "what" are as "wholly suited to each other" as two lovers who cannot determine which first aroused the other's love. The "highly unspeculative understanding" which exists between the two is not an altogether clear one, but who can say how it could be improved?

D. Faith and the Conflict of Passion and Reason

How does Kierkegaard's concept of faith in the Climacus writings fit with the theories of passion outlined in Chapter One?

1. The Regularity Theory: Ryle

Kierkegaard's emphasis on the "how" of faith has certain similarities with Ryle's dispositional analysis. The two are united, at any rate, in what they are against--the "intellectualist legend" that intelligent performance involves merely possessing the proper truths. On the positive side, moreover, they could agree on the paramount necessity for training and practice.

Nevertheless, there is a good deal in Ryle with which Climacus would never agree, and certainly the styles in which the two write are vastly different. Particularly foreign to Kierkegaard is an assumption which seems implicit in Ryle's procedure, that "extroversion is a Good Thing."[53] Whether Ryle

---

[52]*Postscript*, p. 206.

[53]This expression is, of course, not Ryle's, and he would surely not wish to defend it stated in this way. The phrase comes from an article by J. R. Lucas called "The Soul," in *Faith and Logic* (London, 1957), p. 138.

Faith

would want to defend such a notion formally is uncertain; surely the Climacus writings would not. "True inwardness demands absolutely no outward sign," writes Climacus of Religiousness A;[54] and although Kierkegaard with respect to Religiousness B places an ever-increasing stress on the outward sign,[55] he retains throughout his career a strong sense of the ambiguity of any external expression.

If one were to describe Kierkegaard's analysis of the "how" of faith as a "dispositional" theory of that passion, the proviso would have to be added that the dispositions involved are those of people, not products. As Hampshire notes,[56] the analogy between human traits and physical properties such as brittleness or solubility is quite limited. Pressing the analogy too far will lead one to think of human actions in physicalistic terms, as did classical behaviorism; or, taking the opposite tack, to view physical processes in human terms and wind up with--of all things--a kind of animism.

2. The Rationalistic Theory: Spinoza and Peters

Seen against the background of the viewpoint which we have identified in Spinoza and Peters, faith is a peculiar passion indeed. Consider the anomalies which result when the characterizations by Climacus are compared with the polarities of the rationalistic position.

(a) *Faith a "Given" and a Task*: In his own way Climacus combines the points of both the regularity and the rationalistic

---

[54]*Postscript*, p. 370.

[55]This is especially true of the late polemical writings, in which it is argued that the suffering of a "witness for the truth" should be manifest; see *Attack Upon Christendom* (Boston, 1956). Did Kierkegaard earlier think that Christianity produced no externally recognizable sign at all in a man's life? Richard Popkin argues that this was indeed Kierkegaard's characteristic view and the inevitable outcome of his skeptical position. Popkin cites the case of Abraham in *Fear and Trembling*, who cannot even be sure that he himself has faith. See Popkin, "Theological and Religious Skepticism," *Christian Scholar*, XXXIX (June, 1956), p. 157; and "Kierkegaard and Skepticism," *Algemeen Nederlands Tijdschrift voor Wijsbegeerte en Psychologie*, LI (1958, No. 3), p. 140. But probably Abraham might in this book better be taken as a representative of Religiousness A than of Religiousness B.

[56]See *supra*, Chapter One, footnote 29.

theories, but he does not join the two in any synthesis. The *Fragments* places the stress on the "objective" side, that is, on the "condition" or "given" dispositions of faith. No justification is given for the passion of the man for whom "Subjectivity is untruth"; "he *would* do that," since that is what belongs to a "new creature." The *Postscript*, on the other hand, takes up the "subjective" side of the passion of faith and places before the individual the "task of becoming subjective."[57] Faith is not something which can be imposed on the individual, even by the sacred rite of baptism. It is rather the highest task and the most serious responsibility of every human being.

(b) *Faith as Active and Passive*: For the same reasons that one cannot separate out the "given" of faith from the task, one is unable to mark a neat distinction between activity and passivity in this passion. It could be argued that the term "passion" connotes the passive side more than the active. The word is, at any rate, more prominent in the *Fragments* than in the *Postscript*, in which it is supplemented (but not replaced) by "subjectivity" and "inwardness." But Climacus by no means wishes to suggest that faith is not an action.[58]

The combination of activity and passivity which Climacus implicitly recognizes in faith is discussed explicitly with respect to offense, the "unhappy passion" which is the opposite of faith. "All offense is in its deepest root passive," he writes,[59] when it flaunts its strength and wit in derision of the Paradox just as much as when it is paralyzed by suffering. But this passivity does not exclude activity as such:

> ... it is quite possible to distinguish between an active and a passive form of the offended consciousness, if we take care to remember that the passive form is so far active as not to permit itself wholly to be annihilated (for offense is always an act, never

---

[57] This is the title of Chapter One of Part II of the *Postscript*.

[58] Cf. Perry D. LeFevre, *The Prayers of Kierkegaard* (Chicago, 1963), p. 193: "Nor is passion passive; it is active, but the action is all inward. It involves the transformation of the entire existence of the individual."

[59] *Fragments*, p. 61.

Faith 61

an event); and that the active form is always so weak that it cannot free itself from the cross to which it is nailed, or tear the arrow from out its wound."[60] Faith, like offense, is "always an act, never an event."

(c) *Faith with Joy and Suffering*: The Climacus writings say little about what the passion of faith would be in terms of the Spinozistic division between joy (associated with activity and clarity) and suffering.[61] The reticence of Climacus here is fitting, since he does not give himself out to be a Christian[62] and thus does not claim to have a first-hand acquaintance with the Christian life.

Søren Kierkegaard, however, published a volume some years after the *Postscript* had appeared which throws light on the topic. Kierkegaard gives us several specifically Christian discourses on the theme "Joyful Notes in the Midst of Suffering."[63] Joy and suffering together--what a strange combination! The titles of these discourses display further this paradoxical conjunction: "The Joy of it--that the poorer thou dost become, the richer thou canst make others," "The Joy of it--that the weaker thou dost become, the stronger does God become in thee," and "The Joy of it--that Misfortune is Good Fortune."

In order to become convinced of the inadequacy of some traditional philosophical categories for the description of what

---

[60]*Ibid.*, p. 62. The footnote which Climacus appends is also of importance: "The idiom of the language also supports the view that all offense is passive. We say: 'to be offended', which primarily expresses only the state or condition; but we also say, as identical in meaning with the foregoing: 'to take offense', which expresses a synthesis of active and passive. The Greek word is σκανδαλίζεσθαι. This word comes from σκάνδαλον (offense or stumbling-block), and hence means to take offense, or to collide with something. Here the movement of thought is clearly indicated; it is not that offense provokes the collision, but that it meets with a collision, and hence passively, although so far actively as itself to take offense. Hence the Reason is not the discoverer of offense; for the paradoxical collision which the Reason develops in isolation discovers neither the Paradox nor the reaction of offense."

[61]He does speak of these two in the *Postscript*, pp. 404-05, but the context indicates that he is speaking of "Religiousness A" and not of Christianity.

[62]*Ibid.*, p. 545.

[63]*Christian Discourses* (London, 1940), pp. 95-163.

Climacus might mean by the passion of faith, one has only to take that list of titles and ask: How would one explicate this passion in terms of a scheme in which clarity, activity, and joy increased and decreased together? Indeed, it is hard to see how any everyday set of categories could accommodate the passion of faith; which is in a way to state that with respect to faith, subjectivity is untruth.

3. The Analogy Between Faith and Love

The way in which neither traditional philosophical framework which we have discussed is adequate to the passion of faith which Kierkegaard describes in the *Fragments* and the *Postscript* raises the question whether this passion would find a congenial spot in any general theory of the passions. A negative answer to this question would not have troubled Kierkegaard's Climacus, and for good reason. He is not interested in showing that faith as a passion shows patterns common to the species. On the contrary, his concern is with the distinctiveness of this passion, and all his skill is employed to show its idiosyncratic character, so that there can be but one "what" to correspond to such a distinctive "how."

Insofar as Kierkegaard in these works does refer to features which faith has in common with other passions, he does this usually in connection with a very restricted set of passions, and most often with respect to one paradigm case--love. Typical in this regard is the way in which the mutual fit of the paradox and the passion is compared to two lovers who are so wholly suited to each other that their only dispute is "whether he first aroused her passion, or she his."[64] Who will raise the issue of activity and passivity in such a case? The analogy is characteristic. Again and again[65] Kierkegaard draws on imagery from love

---

[64] *Postscript*, p. 206; cf. *supra*, Section C, 2, d.

[65] The best known of these examples, of course, is the story of the king who loved a humble maiden (*Fragments*, pp. 32-42). In some of his last papers Kierkegaard uses the analogy between faith and love again, to illustrate the mistake of trying to have the "what" without the "how":

"In the category of the Absurd, rightly understood, there is therefore nothing terrifying. No, it is precisely the category of courage and of enthusiasm. Take an analogy: Love blinds. It is, after all, a bitter story that one becomes blind. Well, then, you can reduce the blindness a little bit so that (cont...)

to explain aspects of faith, and often we learn that the ambiguities in the concept of faith (as in the above case, between activity and passivity) are ambiguities also within the passion of love.

Kierkegaard's procedure here might be criticized on the grounds that in taking love as his example he has chosen a maverick passion for his paradigm case. For example, the question of justification sounds out of place in the case of love; who demands that romance be reasonable? Nor is this passion any more notable for its regularity than its rationality. But criticism of Kierkegaard on such a basis would miss his point, since he is not setting forth a general theory. All he needs is that the concept of passion be at least a "family resemblance" concept and that love, which is an undoubted case of passion, be a close "relative" to faith.

E. Passion, Knowledge, and Faith

Kierkegaard's discussion of the passion of faith leaves us with a number of questions.

The epitome of the treatment of the concept of faith comes in those sections at the end of the *Postscript* where Climacus makes the statements which are later summarized by Kierkegaard as "If the 'how' is truly given, then the 'what' is also given." When applied to the Christian faith that dictum seems to go too far. For in principle it must be possible to find more than one "what" which could go with any "how," although if the "how" is a highly specific one this may not be attainable in fact. The Christian "how" to which Climacus refers must be a very particular one, if it is still more specific than that of Religiousness A, so perhaps no one is able to imagine a "what" which may accompany the "how" of faith except the Incarnation; but still another "what" for this "how" is logically possible.

---

so that he does not become entirely blind. But beware that reducing the blindness you don't reduce love. True love makes for total blindness.
   "And true faith breathes healthily and blissfully in the Absurd. A weaker faith must peer and speculate just like the weaker love, which lacked the courage to become totally blind, and for that very reason became an enfeebled love, or because it was an enfeebled love, did not become totally blind." X^6 B 79, p. 86. (Fabro, in *Kierkegaard Critique*, p. 183)

The situation, however, is not as bad for Climacus as it appears. For with what categories is one to describe the alternate "what" for the Christian "how"? Since "Subjectivity is truth" (but the truth of a new subjectivity), the categories which can with truth religiously describe the Incarnation must be rooted in the subjectivity, the "how," the "form of life" of the "new creature" in Christ. The *Fragments*, and in particular the "Project of Thought," brings this fact home. If the "what" is not the Incarnation, then the categories in which it is conveyed are also not those of the Christian "how" but are from the "how" of some counterfeit of Christianity--the "how," for example, of the heaven-storming assistant professor who wants to fit Christianity into his speculative schemes, or of the paunchy parson who enjoys delivering sermons on martyrdom, or of his parishioners strolling (of themselves) in Deer Park.

At the same time, Climacus cannot allow that the Incarnation be accessible only to the categories of faith. Indeed, it is essential to the historicity of the Incarnation that it be possible for the faithful to be able to speak of the Incarnation as being the "same" in some sense as certain events which are described also by those who lack faith. But while there is this overlap between the categories of the faithful and the non-faithful, the Christian will insist that the non-Christian, because he lacks the "how," lacks also the categories for fully specifying the "what" in the way the Christian understands it. And this is all that Climacus needs in order to be able to speak of the "mutual fit" of the paradox and the passion.

After this has been said, many questions remain. Some of them are queries about Kierkegaardian scholarship, and these will not be treated further. But others arise out of the issues raised by Climacus' view of faith as involving a "how" of passionate commitment: What are the philosophical possibilities of a dispositional analysis of faith? If the categories of faith are embedded in the "how" of the Christian life, how can Christians communicate to others about their beliefs? The next two chapters will suggest some ways in which these questions can be discussed.

CHAPTER THREE

"KNOWING HOW" AND RELIGIOUS BELIEF

The purpose of this part of the essay is to explore some of the possibilities of a dispositional analysis of knowledge through the categories of "knowing how" and "knowing that," and then to examine some recent attempts by philosophers of religion to apply such categories in discussing the place of knowledge in religious belief.

A. "Knowing How" and "Knowing That"

1. Ryle and "Knowing How"

The distinction between "knowing how" and "knowing that" about which this chapter revolves is one which has already been used above in a number of places. In Climacus' *Fragments* Socratic "knowledge" is shown[1] to have the peculiar feature that it never requires to be learned, never requires to be received as new information. No news is announced, no information is given, through this sort of knowledge. The learner, Socrates insists, knows these matters all the time and only needs to have them dialectically teased out of him. A somewhat parallel treatment of philosophical problems is made by Wittgenstein, who follows the procedure of not setting up any theses but only bringing out more perspicaciously the character of what we knew all along.[2]

But the knowledge thus ascribed to Socrates in the *Fragments* is of a different sort from the kind of knowledge which a man does *not* possess all the time but which he must learn afresh. Kierkegaard in the Climacus writings marks this distinction with two terms for knowledge, "kunnen" and "viden." The first of these can be "directly" communicated as a "what"; the second can only be "indirectly" given in a "how." Even rote-learning may provide a man with a "what," but only practice (often of a prolonged, difficult, and specific sort) can produce a "how."

---

[1]*Fragments*, Chapter One; cf. *supra*, Chapter Two, B: "The 'How' and the 'What'," pp. 43-45.

[2]*Philosophical Investigations* (Oxford, 1958), I, #126-29, 599.

When Gilbert Ryle makes his suggestion[3] concerning "knowing how" and "knowing that," the division of the concept of knowledge recalls Climacus, especially in the contrast between rote-learning and training. In other respects Kierkegaard and Ryle are nearly as unlike in style and concerns as any two philosophers one can name, so that any general comparison is likely to founder. But because Ryle's distinction has been much discussed recently and criticized, an examination of the possibilities and ambiguities of his position may prove helpful in order to gain a fresh vantage-point upon recent philosophers who, like Kierkegaard, fasten upon the "how" as the key factor in religious faith.

The immediate target of Ryle's critique with the "knowing how"/"knowing that" distinction is a view variously identified as "Descartes' myth" or the "intellectualist legend."[4] According to this standpoint, being rational, acting intelligently, and the like, are to be defined in terms of the acquisition of truths. To become rational means that one obtain, by special insight or by some more everyday manner of impartation (the precise mechanics are understandably left unclear), the possession of certain principles; to act intelligently means that one apply these principles when the appropriate situations arise. That people as a matter of fact can often act without any notion of what principles are being applied and yet, by and large, perform quite intelligently does not disturb the theorists of the "intellectualist" tradition at all. These philosophers are perfectly willing to concede, and may even insist, that the principles applied during intelligent action are only "tacitly" known by the person acting. Indeed, not only the principles acted on, but even the fact that they are being applied, may be unknown to the agent and often of supreme indifference to him. The person has been performing in ways of which he is not aware, but which the philosopher exposes through his analysis.

---

[3] "Knowing How and Knowing That," *PAS* (1945-46), 1-16; *Concept of Mind* (New York, 1949), Chapter Two. Cf. Ryle, "Teaching and Training," *The Concept of Education*, ed. R. S. Peters (New York, 1967), pp. 105-19.

[4] *Concept of Mind*, pp. 11, 29.

Ryle's objections to this standpoint, as they are stated in the *Concept of Mind*, are well known:[5]

(1) The assumption that the person in acting rationally possesses unawares a group of principles and judges according to them is an unnecessary one. Of course he may judge by principles, and this is often a commendable procedure, but then we expect him to be able to tell us what these principles are. Moreover, in many undoubted cases of intelligent action, such as swimming, driving a car, or speaking French, we might be surprised if the person *could* state the principles of his action and would not in the least disparage his swimming and the like if he proved incapable of learning the principles (whatever they are).

(2) Not only is the assumption unnecessary, but it may work in the opposite way from that intended and change the whole character of the action. With some actions, to perform them according to set principles may subvert their purpose or even render them entirely ineffectual. The "ars amatoria" may be taken as an example of the first case, while the notable case of the centipede who could walk until he was asked how he did it illustrates the second.

(3) More serious yet is another logical feature of the view criticized, that it leads to a vicious infinite regress. Ryle puts it this way:

> The crucial objection to the intellectualist legend is this. The consideration of propositions is itself an operation of which can be more or less intelligent, less or more stupid. But if for any operation to be intelligently executed, a prior theoretical operation had first to be performed and performed intelligently, it would be a logical impossibility for anyone to break into the circle.[6]

Or one can state the matter more picturesquely by asking about the Cartesian "soul" or whatever "inner" agent it is which executes all the judgments that render actions intelligent. Before the inner man can perform his function he needs to consult the rule-book of principles; but before that performance can be carried out, *his* inner man must consult *his* rule-book, and so

---

[5] *Ibid.*, esp. pp. 25-32.

[6] *Ibid.*, p. 30.

ad infinitum; and until the innermost man has consulted the ultimate rule-book (which can never happen) the actions of none of the members of the chain are intelligent, rational, and the rest.

2. Analyzing "Knowing That" as "Knowing How"

The arguments which Ryle gives are intended to defend the distinction between "knowing how" and "knowing that." The "intellectualist legend" is his way of lumping together the attempts which might be made to subsume all cases of "knowing how" under "knowing that." But what of the opposite possibility, that the cases of "knowing that" might all turn out to be instances of "knowing how"? Ryle's defense here turns out to be a great deal more feeble.

This difficulty in Ryle's distinction was pointed out by Hartland-Swann in 1956.[7] The article agrees with Ryle's analysis of "knowing how" and "knowing that," but argues that, given this analysis, the distinction between the two cannot be maintained. For Ryle upholds and elaborates in many ways the thesis that "knowledge" is a "capacity" verb, and "knowledge" here presumably includes both "knowing how" and "knowing that."[8] But capacities are dispositional and not episodic, and they are improved by practice and training; which means that they belong to "knowing how" rather than "knowing that." Ryle's distinction between "knowing how" and "knowing that" holds only on the superficial level. On further analysis both of them turn out to be "knowing how."

---

[7] "The Logical Status of 'Knowing That'," *Analysis*, XVI/5 (March, 1956), pp. 111-15.

[8] Ryle in fact never states flatly that both "knowing how" and "knowing that" are dispositional concepts, but both what he says about them and his general procedure of analysis with them make it obvious that this is his view. Martin in "On the Reduction of 'Knowing That' to 'Knowing How'," *Language and Concepts in Education*, ed. Smith and Ennis (Chicago, 1961), p. 70, footnote 10, draws this conclusion but notes that Ryle "states that 'knowing how' is a disposition but never makes explicit the 'logical status' of 'knowing that'." Scheffler, ("On Ryle's Theory of Propositional Belief," *JP*, LXV [November 21, 1968], p. 727), on the other hand, believes that Ryle (in the critical passage, *Concept of Mind*, pp. 133-34) is referring to "knowing that" rather than "knowing how" as dispositional; but since the examples of "know" which Ryle gives on the following page are instances where the term applies to skills such as tying clove hitches, the point is clearer to Scheffler than it is to me.

To this argument Robert Ammerman replied in a later issue of *Analysis* with two main objections:[9]

(1) The first of these is that "knowing how" may be correct or not, whereas we only say that someone "knows that" x is the case if he can state the case *correctly*.[10] Hartland-Swann's answer is that neither "knowing how" nor "knowing that" can be incorrect, and this not for any empirical reason, but because "know" in any form marks an achievement and if we wish to speak of a procedure which may fail we shall have to introduce another term altogether.[11]

(2) Even if Ryle and Hartland-Swann did wish to make "knowing how" by definition something which cannot be incorrect and which always achieves the statement of what is the case, Ammerman argues, they cannot succeed, since this is more than the concept of "knowing how" can perform. "Knowing how" only tells about the speaker and his capacities and thus cannot, however much detail is provided, tell us whether what the speaker says is true of the facts of the case.[12] To this Hartland-Swann replies that "know that" does indeed involve more than statements about the knower, but this does not make "know that" something else than a capacity verb.

In order to make a valid know-claim I must have evidence, and this evidence frequently consists in having

---

[9] "A Note on 'Knowing That'," *Analysis*, XVII/2 (December, 1956), pp. 30-32.

[10] *Ibid.*, p. 31. Ammerman's objection here is based on Hartland-Swann's phraseology, but the question is not merely a verbal one. A similar objection is raised by Ernest Gellner ("Knowing How and Validity," *Analysis*, XII/2 [December, 1951], pp. 25-35, esp. p. 31) to the "knowing how" claim and particularly to the use of it by Stephen Toulmin (cf. footnote 25, *infra*).

[11] Hartland-Swann, "Knowing That--A Reply to Mr. Ammerman," *Analysis*, XVII/3 (January, 1957), pp. 69-71. Some refinements in the definition of "knowing that" as an achievement concept are developed by E. M. Adams in "On Knowing That," *PQ*, VIII (October, 1958), pp. 300-06, and (in consultation with Ryle) by Alan R. White in "Thinking That and Knowing That," *PQ*, XI (1961), pp. 68-73, esp. pp. 71-73.

[12] Ammerman, "A Note," pp. 31-32. An argument very close to this also forms the concluding part of the discussion of "knowing how" by Betty Powell in "Knowing How and Knowing That," Chapter Two of *Knowledge of Actions* (London, 1967), pp. 28-30.

looked at or listened or read something authoritative. Now verbs like "looking," "listening," and "reading" are episodic; they report occurrences. "Knowing," however, when it means knowing *that*, does not report any occurrence--it implies a capacity. Hence, although know-claims are usually *based on* occurrences such as looking, hearing, and so forth, knowing *that* statements have a very different logic from statements reporting the occurrences on which they are based.[13]

3. Martin: Kinds of "Knowing How"

In terms of the definitions accepted and the principles employed, Hartland-Swann's argument is about as conclusive as any philosophical demonstration is likely to be. Where capacities are matters of "knowing how," the capacity which is "knowing that" turns out on analysis to be a kind of "knowing how." And with this analysis the original distinction between "knowing that" and "knowing how" dissolves.[14] Yet surely some sort of distinction is needed between such cases as "I know that the cat is on the mat" and "I know how to swim"; and if the distinction is not one of disposition vs. episode, then it should be marked in some other way.

An effort in this direction has been made by Jane Roland Martin.[15] She agrees with Hartland-Swann that "knowing that" can

---

[13]Hartland-Swann, "A Reply," pp. 70-71.

[14]The argument has been challenged from another direction by Betty Powell, *Knowledge of Actions*, p. 23. Powell grants that knowing is not episodic in the sense of requiring an internal act of apprehending truths; but she proposes that the term "know" be restricted to those cases of knowing in which some truths or rules would be relevant. It is not clear whether she means (1) that rules or truths could be relevant even if the person were unaware of them and of their relevance, or (2) that certain episodic elements ("I saw," "I heard," etc.) are among the criteria for applying the term "knowing" to a certain disposition. The first does not seem to be her position, since she does not want to say that of the person who fortuitously acts according to certain principles that he "knows"; while the second makes substantially the same distinction which Hartland-Swann draws between dispositions which involve episodic events and those which do not. Thus there is no reason why Hartland-Swann could not accept her proposal for the use of the term "know," so long as it is kept clear that this is a proposal. But evidently she means her remark to be more than just a proposal, since she goes on to suggest that also with some clear cases of skills (e.g., marksmanship, p. 29) the decisive conditions are "knowing that."

[15]Jane Roland [Martin], "On the Reduction of 'Knowing That' to 'Knowing How'," *Language and Concepts in Education*, ed. Smith and Ennis (Chicago, 1961), pp. 59-71.

"Knowing How" and "Knowing That" 71

be analyzed into "knowing how" capacities, but she goes on to suggest, very convincingly, that there remain important distinctions *within* the area of "knowing how." She distinguishes between

    (1) "knowing how" to perform skills, such as how to swim or how to speak French, on the one hand; and

    (2) "knowing how" to state propositions of a factual nature such as being able to give testimony in court as to what happened in a murder which one has witnessed.

"The feature which distinguishes these two kinds of capacities from each other," she says, is *"practice."*[16] One learns how to swim by practicing swimming, but one does not learn to give testimony about a murder in that way.

Once Martin has made the initial distinction, four categories within "knowing how" also come into view, and it is difficult to know where to stop.

    (1) The first class centers around skills such as swimming and speaking French, both of which require practice,[17] while

    (2) the second grouping centers around the capacity to state facts, such as the details of a murder.

But does it not require practice to become a good witness to a murder? Might there not be a difference in skill between a trained observer, a policeman for example, and a flurried spinster who hardly ever comes out on the street? Martin discusses this sort of question in a footnote[18] and grants that a variety

---

[16] *Ibid.*, p. 62. Italics in original.

[17] To the objection that it is possible that someone should without practicing jump into the pool and paddle capably away, Martin replies (*ibid.*, p. 63) quite properly that "We cannot deny that he is swimming but we might well wish to deny that he knows how to swim." Martin does not take this further and ask what would happen if people regularly leaped into pools and swam like Olympic champions, but there is no good answer to questions of this sort. All one can say is that, if this happened frequently and in many sports and skills, our conceptual distinctions might be quite different from those they are.

[18] *Ibid.*, pp. 70-71, footnote 12.

of experience and some drill might make someone a better witness, but "the effort involved in learning and hence knowing that such and such is the case cannot be considered practice in *stating* that particular fact or *answering* a particular question."[19] This qualification buttresses the distinction satisfactorily for the moment, but creates additional difficulty with the second example of the "knowing how"-through-practice category, knowing how to speak French. For it is not the case that a person must have practiced every use of an expression in French in every situation before he is able to employ it correctly. Skill in languages is not exactly like skill in swimming. Once one has learned to do the breast stroke, for instance, it only remains to do the same thing over and over as quickly as possible; whereas when one learns French, one does not first practice all the possible word uses and then simply repeat them at a faster and faster clip (though sometimes it may sound this way!). Rather one "knows how" to speak French in a conversation even though one has never practiced *this particular* phrase for *this particular* situation. If this were not the case, one could not write new French poems, plays, or academic monographs, but each performance of French speaking would be as like the last as are the questions and answers of a tourist in Paris who goes completely by his "phrase book."

After Martin's practice criterion has been challenged in this way, each of her examples for the first two classifications--swimming, speaking French, and reporting a murder--falls into a different category:

(1) Swimming (which requires practice of particular motions);

(1.5) Speaking French (which requires practice, but not just the repetition of a stock of words); and

(2) Reporting a murder (which requires practice, but not for this particular murder).

The third classification which Martin offers is the least convincing. This is:

---

[19]*Ibid.* Italics in original.

(3) "Knowing how the accident happened."[20] Surely Martin has been misled here by the verbal form when she classifies this as a kind of "knowing how." Of course if all knowledge is somehow "knowing how," then so is this, but the conjunction of the words "know" and "how" in this case does not by itself give any indication that there is a skill or capacity being exercised. If one prefers, one can make this situation the paradigm of a separate type of capacity, and then go on to cite as parallel categories "know whether," "know who," "know whom," "know when," and so on indefinitely. Yet it is hard to see what point is served by multiplying classifications in this way.

(4) The last grouping in the article has to do with knowing rules of conduct, as in "Johnny knows that he should." One way of taking this statement is according to "knowing how" type 2, above.[21] But a more usual way of understanding it, she thinks, would be that it shows that "Johnny has internalized a certain rule of conduct or moral code" and that we may expect that the appropriate behavior "will, quite generally, be exhibited."[22] In the latter sense there is no "knowing how" involved, since "knowing how" is a *capacity* dispositional concept (that is, it need only be occasionally exhibited), whereas Johnny's moral behavior is a *tendency* disposition: it must always or usually be exhibited or we shall deny that Johnny has internalized the rule of conduct.[23] But Martin's use of the category of "knowing how" has by this point in her analysis become so broad that it is hard to keep the category from being applied to Johnny simply on the grounds that his capacity is usually rather than occasionally exercised. In the end she suggests that also Johnny's case might turn out on analysis to be a "knowing how," but she has to amend Ryle's notion of "knowing how" to include both capacity and tendency concepts.[24]

---

[20] *Ibid.*, pp. 64-65.

[21] *Ibid.*, pp. 66-67.

[22] *Ibid.*, p. 67.

[23] This distinction is Ryle's; see *Concept of Mind*, p. 131.

[24] Martin, "On the Reduction of 'Knowing That'," p. 67.

(5) How far can Martin's application of "knowing how" be expanded? A severe test of the ability of the "knowing how" aspect to elucidate the whole concept of knowledge comes in the case of logical and mathematical truths, which have been the stronghold of Cartesianism. A contribution along these lines was made by Stephen Toulmin shortly after Ryle first made the "knowing how"/"knowing that" distinction.[25] Toulmin suggests that "knowing how" may be a way of explicating something of what philosophers have meant when they talked about an *a priori*. Instead of looking on the *a priori* as a sort of insight into

---

[25] Stephen Toulmin, "A Defense of 'Synthetic Necessary Truth'," *Mind*, LVIII (April, 1949), pp. 164-77. For a contrary viewpoint see Gellner, footnote 10, *supra*. Toulmin develops his notion in *Uses of Argument* (Cambridge, 1964), esp. pp. 188-210.

A diverting demonstration that there is an irreducible element of "knowing how" even in logic and mathematics is provided by Lewis Carroll in his apocryphal account of a dialogue between Achilles and the Tortoise. The Tortoise takes from Euclid two simple premises and their conclusion (labeled A, B, and Z respectively), and asks what will happen if he accepts A and B but denies that the sequence "If A and B then Z" (label this hypothetical "C") is valid. Without C the demonstration is not complete; so we demand that the Tortoise accept C as well. But then we learn that there is a new sequence involved, "If A, B and C, then Z" (label this hypothetical "D") before the Tortoise must accept Z. Suppose, however, that the stubborn Tortoise accepts A, B, C, and D but *still* refuses to accept Z. Achilles replies triumphantly: "Then Logic would take you by the throat, and *force* you to do it! Logic would tell you 'You can't help yourself. Now that you've accepted A and B and C and D, you *must* accept Z.' So you've no choice, you see." But alas for Achilles; he is unable to stop the trend and months later when the narrator returns he is still trying to make the deduction complete by adding hypotheticals. ("What the Tortoise Said to Achilles," *The Complete Works of Lewis Carroll* [New York, n.d.], pp. 1225-30).

What has forced this paradox upon Achilles? Is Euclid incomplete? Or does logic take one by the throat? Neither one. The practice of inferring is a "how," a human activity. The hypothetical, C, does not indicate an additional premise which one needs in order to derive Z from A and B; seeing the point of this proof *is* drawing the conclusion Z. Making the proof more "complete" by transforming this "how" into part of the "what" of the premises simply makes the proof endless, for without a "how" no amount of "what" will suffice. Propositions and principles, however numerous and sophisticated, do not draw conclusions by themselves; people must draw them. This does not mean, however, that there is a mysterious background beyond logic. The "how" can, as the Tortoise showed, be formalized in the "what"; but unless there is an end to this formalizing and an unformalized "how" remaining, the proof will be unable to begin.

principles, or taking the contrary standpoint that it is merely
a matter of definitions, he recommends that we view it as a matter of "understanding the nature of the subject-matter," which
is "as much 'knowing how....' or 'knowing what it is to....'
as it is 'knowing that....'."[26]

4. The Category of "Knowing How"

Factual, practical, moral, mathematical, logical--the kinds
of knowledge which have just been discussed in terms of "knowing
how" cover a wide spectrum. Like many other philosophical theses,
the notion that many, if not all, kinds of knowledge can be analyzed in terms of "knowing how" becomes pointless when it is
pushed too far. The category of "knowing how" becomes trivial
if it means no more than that the capacity for human knowledge
is a human capacity; whereas if the idea is carried to the other
extreme, to make of all knowing simply a "knack," it is clearly
wrongheaded.

What is the purpose, then, of employing the concept of
"knowing how" in this way? It serves as a reminder of the skills
which are involved in the art of coming to know, skills which require practice which often must extend over a long period of time.
The point may seem too obvious to mention, but (as in map-reading
with names which are printed in such large type that they span
continents) it is sometimes more difficult to see than matters
which are more minute.

For this situation we can learn from Chesterton's case of
the "invisible man." In a detective story by that title G. K.
Chesterton gives the classic account of an "impossible" crime.
The witnesses all agree that no one entered or left the room of
the crime, and the witnesses are not in collusion, and yet a
murder has been committed. The police are almost ready to call
the murder impossible, and some are hinting at supernatural
agencies, when Father Brown elicits the fact that a letter has
been delivered and deduces that there has been a visitor--the
postman. The witnesses had all seen him and yet they had not
lied. He was "invisible" to them, not because he was furtive
but because his visit was such a routine and everyday performance that no one would notice it unless attention was specifically drawn to the fact.

---

[26]Toulmin, "A Defense," p. 176.

"Knowing how" capacities are "obvious" in that way. Practicing counting or telling time, learning to draw valid conclusions, taking training in reporting accurately--together with countless other ways of developing rational skills--require immense and prolonged effort. Yet these practices are so much a part of our everyday life that they are easy to overlook, so that when someone confronts us abruptly with the question "Well, how do you *know*?" we can only stare blankly in reply. That is the point at which some philosopher may trot out his apparatus to account for and validate our knowledge--para-mechanical processes, cognitions, volitions, judgments, structures of consciousness, and who knows what else--all of which is required, we are told, even though apart from the philosopher's analysis we should not even have suspected the existence of these items. A few hardy skeptics can always be found, moreover, who will doubt that the speculative apparatus can do the trick and will conclude that human knowledge is impossible. The best answer to both the speculative and the skeptical philosophers is to remind ourselves that their proposals are unnecessary. The "invisible man" who comes to know through practices acquired from constant training, so routine that it goes unnoticed, can and does adequately fill the position of knower. No "ghost in the machine" need apply!

B. Problems in Using "Knowing How" as a Category in Religion

For the remainder of the chapter we shall examine a few contemporary applications of dispositional theories to the problem of religious knowledge and relate them to the Climacean concept of Christian faith. The philosophers will include Paul F. Schmidt, who has recently made a very sketchily outlined proposal for applying the "knowing how"/"knowing that" distinction in religion, together with R. B. Braithwaite and Kai Nielsen, who have put forward parallel views.

1. Schmidt

In an article entitled "Knowing-How in Religion"[27] Paul F. Schmidt outlines a proposal for treating religious claims along "how"/"that" lines. He begins by drawing a sharp distinction between "knowing that" and "knowing how." "To 'know that'," he

---

[27]*Religious Humanism*, II (Spring, 1968), pp. 80-84.

Problems 77

says, "is to possess a belief that such-and-such is the case and to possess the evidence which constitutes sufficient support for that belief."[28] "Knowing how," on the other hand, is the possession of a skill learned by practice, and because this kind of knowledge does not involve assertions, evidence is not relevant for it.

> The crucial point for us is that *knowing-how* does not involve assertions that such and such is the case and yet such statements can be judged correct or incorrect.... *Knowing-how* can occur without any descriptive assertions about states of affairs even though some prescriptive rules may be involved.[29]

Readers of Ryle and his critics will not be surprised at the general terms of this distinction, though they may well be puzzled at the sharpness of the division and by the cavalier manner in which Schmidt dismisses in a footnote[30] the question whether "knowing that" can be reduced to "knowing how."

On the basis of this division Schmidt goes on to deny that religious statements are any sort of assertions ("knowing that") but are rather part of practices ("knowing how") which are designed to produce certain "feelings, moods, emotions, or attitudes." Prayer and meditation, for example, are skills developed in order to create and enhance calm, courage and resolution.[31] When one asks "To whom am I praying?" one is putting an improper "knowing that" question about a "knowing how" sort of knowledge. Not surprisingly, then, Schmidt goes on to describe theological claims as mistakes arising from a confusion of "knowing how" with "knowing that." The concepts of divine omniscience and benevolence are used to illustrate his point.

> God's omniscience tells us how to live a life in continuous search for the rational solution of problems. Omniscience prescribes such dispositions for performance as being intellectual, being curious, seeking solutions, respecting knowing, communicating knowledge, combatting falsehood, and striving for truth. God's omniscience is a way to sum up a large part of how we are to live. The

---

[28] *Ibid.*, p. 80.

[29] *Ibid.*, p. 81.

[30] *Ibid.* Also footnote 4, p. 84.

[31] *Ibid.*, p. 81.

> *knowing-how* of religion is primarily directed toward
> *knowing-how* to live. To claim that God is benevolent
> tells us how to live by being kind to others, of
> sharing and loving all people, of giving, of follow-
> ing one's moral convictions, of being helped, guided
> and protected.[32]

His argument, in short, is that in theology "knowing how" statements have been misleadingly couched in "knowing that" terminology, and that the actual function of theological claims is "to
provide *knowing-how* attitudes for a way of life."[33]

One thing which stands out clearly in the article is that
the "way of life" commended by religious statements is not at all
peculiar to religious people but represents a consensus of the
values, attitudes, and moods of which people may be expected to
approve. Even such an apparently tough case as "I know that my
redeemer liveth" turns out on analysis to be just a way to point
a general moral.

> This statement sums up a way of behavior that is
> confident in the face of possible mistakes and lack
> of success. We know how to act with confidence and
> that such a way of action has proved effective. It
> is couched in a descriptive language built from a
> story woven in beauty, for its better functioning
> as *knowing-how*.[34]

The "know how" and the acceptance for this "way of life" may be
taken for granted; "We know how to act ... and that such a way
of life has proved effective."

Although Schmidt's use of the "knowing how"/"knowing that"
distinction is an unusual one, it is worthwhile noting that
neither his picture of the function of religious statements nor
the conclusion he reaches is dependent upon the use of that terminology. In an earlier volume and an article[35] Schmidt has in
fact built up a similar analysis drawing heavily from A. J. Ayer[36]

---

[32] *Ibid.*, pp. 83-84.

[33] *Ibid.*, p. 84.

[34] *Ibid.*

[35] *Religious Knowledge* (Glencoe, 1961); "Is There Religious Knowledge?" *JP*, LV (June 19, 1958), pp. 529-38.

[36] Schmidt does not want to be bound by the Logical Positivists, but he insists that "their doctrine is a fire of purifica-
tion." (*Religious Knowledge*, p. 46).

along with what he calls "Logical Empiricism," and chastened by the principle that "the meaning of a statement is a function of its use."[37] His analysis runs along long-familiar lines: religious knowledge is not simply formal (as in logic or mathematics) or factual (as in natural science) or ethical; rather, the function of religion is the attainment of certain pervasive "attitudes" (i.e., dispositions to behave in human relations) which are based on beliefs which have been justified in non-religious areas, particularly ethics.[38] Both the earlier "dispositional" and the later "knowing how" approaches come to the same conclusion and in nearly the same way: religion tells us nothing about what is or ought to be, but merely serves to promote attitudes, dispositions, or "ways of life" which are certified on non-religious grounds.

Nevertheless, there are some ways in which the "knowing how" presentation makes plainer than the more detailed earlier writings the nature of Schmidt's argument. The distance between Schmidt and a philosopher like Ryle could not be more evident than when Schmidt tries to make his argument in Ryle's terminology. Distinctions which are flexible and suggestive in Ryle become hard and fast in the application by Schmidt. Prayer, for example, is assigned by Schmidt not to the realm of "assertion" but to the task of producing certain feelings, moods, emotions, or attitudes--or, briefly, not to the cognitive but to the emotive and conative functions. But this either/or sounds more like Ayer than it does Ryle, who had, besides, no love for the cognitive-conative-emotive divisions of faculty psychology. Nor does Schmidt seem to have profited from the discussion of Ryle's work by Hartland-Swann and others.[39] If "knowing that" can be

---

[37]"Is There Religious Knowledge?" p. 529; cf. *Religious Knowledge*, p. 75.

[38]*Religious Knowledge*, esp. pp. 77-78, 83, 111; "Is There Religious Knowledge?" pp. 537-38.

[39]From all appearances Schmidt is simply not very interested in the refinements in the concept of "knowing how" which are suggested by Hartland-Swann, Martin, and others. (Indeed, he does not even bother to cite them correctly.) He simply wishes to state in a newer terminology the critique which he had made before. In doing this, however, he makes a suggestion about the applicability of the "knowing how" notion to religion which could be even more useful than he seems to realize, and which might, in fact, begin to undermine the simplicity of the framework within which he works.

analyzed as a form of "knowing how," then the distinction on which Schmidt rests his case disappears. And even when differences are discovered within "knowing how," they are much too subtle, various, and overlapping to allow them to be used as a simple formula for separating out assertions on the one hand from emotions and attitudes on the other.

2. Braithwaite

Apart from his "knowing how" article Schmidt's writing is very close to the earlier and better-known position established by R. B. Braithwaite in his Eddington Lecture for 1955 entitled "An Empiricist's View of the Nature of Religious Belief."[40] Braithwaite, too, begins from the formal/factual distinction,[41] and by the "use principle" allows for ethical knowledge,[42] and finally describes religion in terms of a "way of life."[43]

While the two proposals are remarkably similar there is a greater emphasis by Braithwaite on the "conative"[44] side of religious statements. But Braithwaite does bring up four points of distinction between the religious and moral utterances:

(1) Whereas the ethical statements may be taken in isolation as statements of policy, religious utterances are representative of a system which specifies a "way of life,"[45] and, specifically for Christians, the "agapeistic way of life,"[46] as stated, for example, in I Corinthians thirteen.

(2) Religious teachings are frequently given in concrete examples rather than in abstractions--"of how to behave, for

---

[40] Reprinted in: *Christian Ethics and Contemporary Philosophy*, ed. I. T. Ramsey (London, 1966), pp. 53-73.

[41] *Ibid.*, p. 55. He divides what Schmidt calls "factual" into two parts, "statements about particular matters of empirical fact" and "scientific hypotheses and other general empirical statements."

[42] *Ibid.*, p. 58.

[43] *Ibid.*, pp. 61-63.

[44] *Ibid.*, p. 60.

[45] *Ibid.*, p. 62.

[46] *Ibid.*, p. 63.

instance, if one meets a man set upon by thieves on the way to Jericho."[47]

(3) Religious teachings regulate not only external but also internal behavior; they provide a "resolution to feel" as well as a "resolution to act," not just an "agapeistic way of life" but also an "agapeistic frame of mind."[48]

(4) Religious teachings are associated with thinking of stories, which may be considered true or false or even inconsistent with each other,[49] and which do not logically justify the intended course of action but which are only "psychologically" and "causally" connected with it.[50]

The last of these points represents the sharpest difference between morality and religion.

> A moral belief is an intention to behave in a certain way: a religious belief is an intention to behave in a certain way (a moral belief) together with the entertainment of certain stories associated with the intention in the mind of the believer.[51]

This statement, however, makes the cleft between morality and religion look wider than it is. Since both realms are constrained from deducing "ought" from "is"[52] the stories which are used in religious instruction function as causes but not as reasons for the "way of life." Since the use of a moral or religious assertion is not to justify a course of action but to declare one's intention to follow it, it is inappropriate to ask what the reason for following this policy may be.

> What is the reason for my doing what I think I ought to do? The answer ... is that, since my thinking that I ought to do the action is my intention to do it if possible, the reason why I do the action is simply that I intend to do it, if possible.[53]

---

[47] *Ibid.*, p. 64.

[48] *Ibid.*, pp. 64-65.

[49] *Ibid.*, p. 70.

[50] *Ibid.*, p. 71.

[51] *Ibid.*

[52] See, for example, Braithwaite's reply to I. T. Ramsey, *ibid.*, p. 93.

[53] *Ibid.*, pp. 60-61.

It is hard to see how Braithwaite's scheme will allow one to discuss and evaluate the claims of religion *or* morality. His position has the advantage he claims for it, that it does not derive the justification of moral claims from empirical data; but in making this break it seems to cut itself off from any means of justifying moral or religious claims at all. If one is asked to justify a moral assertion, but simply repeatedly and insistently replies "The reason that I intend to do it is that I intend to do it if possible," the normal understanding of this answer is that one dismisses the whole problem of justifying the claim and regards the demand as impertinent besides.

Braithwaite's proposal has been one of the most hotly debated of any in contemporary philosophy of religion. In the immediately ensuing discussion, Braithwaite makes certain statements to put his article in a more defensible posture. He insists, for example, that he "never for a moment thought that the positive account I gave in the lecture is the whole truth about religious belief,"[54] and he mentions that mystical experience in particular requires further treatment. A more important concession appears to be made in the statement that

> ... the efficacy of the Christian set of stories in promoting a Christian way of life has in the past depended, and will doubtless continue to depend, upon many of the type (1) [i.e., strictly historical] statements being believed on reasonable grounds to be true.[55]

But this remark only applies to a very limited set of Christian stories, and it does not, moreover, allow more than a psychological, causal connection between the stories and the faith. Christians generally do accept these stories as true on historical grounds, he is saying, but they might just as well do it on other grounds or not accept their truth at all.

Can religious statements be evaluated in their own right, and do they need first be shown to be analogous to beliefs from other areas, moral or other? One of Braithwaite's critics, D. M. MacKinnon, appeals for a broader conception of the philosopher's task, so that its scope would include the mysteries of faith

---

[54] *Ibid.*, p. 88.

[55] *Ibid.*, p. 91.

considered from *within* the prayer life of the individual thinker. MacKinnon asks:

> ... why should not that life include as part of its discipline a deliberate engagement with the tremendous, even impenetrable mysteries of faith, as they are conveyed in the creeds?[56]

Braithwaite replies:

> Now it is part of the philosophical *askesis* always to be puzzled about something, just as it is the empiricist's burden to hold all his beliefs as subject to further correction. But is it the duty of a philosopher, even of a philosopher of religion, to focus his vocational anguish on to, for example, the hypostatic union rather than on to the relationships between language, thought, and action? Here, surely, are "mysteries" enough (and not, perhaps, completely "impenetrable") to satisfy the most ascetic of philosophers on the path to perfection.[57]

The "mysteries" of language, thought, and action are enough for Braithwaite. Although he cannot finally untangle them, he does not dismiss them but continues to grapple with their difficulties in all his work. This is the proper attitude for a professor of mind and morals to take. But is it appropriate for him to demand of a philosopher in another area and with another set of traditional puzzles, that these other "mysteries" be reformulated in terms of Braithwaite's favorite mysteries of language, thought, and action, and then either handled in these reformulated terms or dismissed? It would seem that this procedure succumbs to just the danger--of disinterest in the persistent problems in a given area of philosophy--against which a philosopher writing in an area outside of his own field would most rigorously have to guard himself.

3. Nielsen

The flurry of articles on the philosophy of religion which has issued from the pen of Kai Nielsen belongs in many respects in the tradition of the views which have just been discussed. The pattern of Braithwaite and Schmidt, however, has been dressed up in terminology more flamboyant even than Ayer's; and, also

---

[56] *Ibid.*, p. 81.

[57] *Ibid.*, p. 92.

like Ayer, there is a tendency to dismiss religious belief in short order by calling it a form of "emotive" expression.

Nielsen's position is most completely stated in one of his earliest articles on the topic, "On Speaking of God" (1962).[58] Leaving aside the unlikely notion that religious statements might be like those in logic and mathematics, Nielsen goes on by means of the "use" principle to ask whether the function of religious statements is to make factual assertions or whether it is to express "basic commitments or decisions."[59] Like Braithwaite and Schmidt, Nielsen finds that religious statements include many which are basic commitments disguised as factual assertions.[60] But unlike his immediate predecessors, and like Ayer, he maintains that religious statements cannot dispense with the apparently factual element which provides them with their emotive force.[61] Or, to put the point in Nielsen's own typically

---

[58]*Theoria*, XXVIII (1962, Part 2), pp. 110-37. Other articles of this sort by Nielsen include: "'Christian Positivism' and the Appeal to Religious Experience" (vs. John Wilson), *JR*, XLII (October, 1962), pp. 248-61; "Eschatological Verification," (vs. John Hick), *Canadian Journal of Theology*, IX (1963), pp. 271-81; "God and Verification Again" (vs. Mavrodes), *Canadian Journal of Theology*, XI (1965), pp. 135-41; "Religious Perplexity and Faith," *The Crane Review*, VIII (Fall, 1965), pp. 1-17; "On Fixing the Reference Range of God" (vs. Gareth Matthews and I. M. Crombie), *Religious Studies*, II (October, 1966). These articles consist mainly of attacks on the proposals of other men which he mounts from the position he established in the *Theoria* article. A few other articles which he directs against a position he calls "fideism" will be referred to in the next chapter of this essay.

[59]*Theoria*, p. 111.

[60]*Ibid.*, pp. 118-19, point #3.

[61]"To be receptive to an I-sentence involves being emotionally entangled in one way or another with the ideological claim made by the sentence in question. The same is true for those who use God-sentences to make claims about God. Russell and Sartre *vehemently deny* there is a God, Marcel and Barth *passionately affirm* there is a God, and Jaspers and James experience the *torture* of doubt. Pent-up emotional energies go into these claims pro and con." *Ibid.*, p. 128; italics in original. At the conclusion of the article he asks: "When a Theist uses a God-sentence, what cognitive or intellectual meaning can he assign to it beyond the meaning which I have claimed here by analyzing God-sentences after the fashion of I-sentences? Is not the rest sound and fury denoting next to nothing though expressing the deepest and most precious of human concerns?" *Ibid.*, p. 137.

colorful vocabulary, they are "genuine bastards" which provide "oomph" for normative claims.[62]

When Nielsen cannot find some more pejorative expression for the combination of factual and normative in religious statements he calls them "pseudo-factual," "ideological," or "I-sentences."[63] This puts them in the same group with statements such as "Men were created free though everywhere they are in chains" and "All men possess an all-pervasive and ineradicable tendency to sin." But unlike these other "ideological" expressions, which can be de-mythologized into their factual and normative components, religious statements cannot.[64] For while the non-religious ideological statements have a different though "appropriate" use (as a "straightforward moral judgment" or a "vague empirical generalization," for example), the religious statements about God have no alternative "appropriate" sense.[65] Here Nielsen parts company with Braithwaite and Schmidt, and insists that the religious "what" is indissolubly wedded to the "how" and any attempt to separate the two will simply destroy them both.

Nielsen's position leaves many questions unanswered. We should like to know in what way religious statements are *formally* different from other ideological statements. All ideological

---

[62]*Ibid.*, p. 135.

[63]*Ibid.*, pp. 118-25 on I-sentences. The use of this argument, usually with expressions such as "ideological" or "pseudo-factual," is a common factor in those articles cited *supra* in footnote 58.

[64]"The normative aspect of certain crucial theistic utterances cannot be intelligibly made without the accompanying assertional claims. The normative aspect of certain Christian utterances is not just moral but is, in addition, an expression of commitment to a Person, where the very sense of 'Person' involves the very conceptual oddities of theistic belief that we have discussed. 'Men were created free though everywhere they are in chains' and 'All men possess an all-pervasive and ineradicable tendency to sin' can be de-mythologized and the moral judgment implicit in them is intelligible without its delusory ideological support.... But if we try to de-mythologize theistic utterances we do not succeed if, à la Braithwaite, we translate them into moral utterances associated with parables which need only be entertained, for the non-assertive element does not consist solely in the expression of moral principles, it consists also in an expression of commitment to a 'Person'. In Christian theism we have a doubly difficult time for the commitment is to a kind of 'God-man'." *Ibid.*, pp. 131-32.

[65]*Ibid.*, p. 132.

statements must be translated into other statements which are different from the originals; but the non-religious statements have an "appropriate" alternative, whereas the religious do not. But what does "appropriate" mean here? "Appropriate" to what? To the original statement? But that statement is of a different type altogether. To the situation of the person? But who decides such a matter? If it is Nielsen himself, he should have no quarrel with Braithwaite and Schmidt, who provide a translation of religious expressions into different terms which fits easily into a general secular morality. Nielsen does not agree with Braithwaite, but he is unable to make a case against him and show that religious ideological statements are formally different from non-religious ones. Both religious and non-religious ideologies have their "accompanying myth or obscurantist claims," Nielsen agrees.[66] Both will change their sense radically if translated into factual or normative claims. Both will lose much of their power to compel when so translated. There may yet be a formal difference between religious and non-religious ideologies about which Nielsen has not told us, but until that distinction is provided they must be treated in the same way.

Once it is established that Nielsen's argument is in effect directed against all ideological statements it becomes easier to assess his claim. He has staked his case on a fight against "ideology" in all its forms, a battle cry which he has picked up from Daniel Bell and others.[67] Since his target is so broad he will not lack for opposition. Chomsky and others have already taken on Bell and the whole idea of a value-free science. But the most serious "opposition" will come from the inner instability of the notion itself. For what could be more ironical than conferences, committees, and manifestos created to promote the idea that ideologies should be banished from society--what, indeed, could be more ideological? Nielsen's strident tone and his call for the end of ideology and the end of theism make him particularly vulnerable to the accusation that he is the

---

[66] *Ibid.*

[67] He acknowledges the debt on p. 136, *ibid.*, footnotes 30 and 31.

Problems 87

ideologue he castigates.[68] It is a situation made to order for
a gadfly; any other critique would take the non-ideological
ideology too seriously.

There is in any case no reason for any religious apologist
to take a special departmental interest in the outcome of the
campaign to outlaw ideology in the sciences and humanities. While
religion would undoubtedly be one victim of the process, the opponents of ideology will be so busy de-mythologizing the fields of
social science, philosophy, literary criticism, and the like, that
they are not likely to get around to religion for some time. Think
of the task of de-mythologizing just one philosopher, such as Hegel, and reducing his thoughts to straightforward moral judgments
and vague empirical generalizations!

What may particularly attract the attention of the philosopher of religion in Nielsen's proposal is a subordinate but important point he makes, that there is no distinctive religious
"how." "The non-Neanderthal believer and the non-believer," he
writes, "have the same expectations about happenings on earth."[69]
Apparently he wishes to maintain that everyone can understand the
"how" of religion but no one can understand the "what." Sometimes
he speaks as if one had to decide on the truth of the "what" first,
apart from the "how."[70] But he does not have to state his case
in that way, and he can agree with Climacus that if the "how" is
given the "what" is also given. There is in the final analysis
no distinctively religious "how," and therefore the appearance
of a distinctive "what" such as the God-man must be a deception.
Religious people may speak and act differently in some respects,
but basically they share the same "how" as other educated modern
men--the same expectations, the same trust in science, the same
calculus of values. And where there might be variations from
the mean in the religious "how," it is very little trouble for
the person without emotional involvement in religion to pick up
the operations involved.[71]

---

[68] As he recognizes somewhat to his embarrassment on pp.
135-36, *ibid.*

[69] *Ibid.*, p. 128.

[70] "Religious Perplexity and Faith," *Crane Review*, VIII
(Fall, 1965), p. 6.

[71] "Even a person with no emotional involvements at all could
understand the non-evaluative 'cosmological' claim made (cont...)

4. Variations in the Dispositional Analysis of Religious Belief

On this last point, concerning the fact that everyone can understand religion because everyone can share the "how," Nielsen cites Kierkegaard in the Climacus writings.[72] Is then the "understanding" of religious statements so easy? One can almost hear the derisive hoots which Climacus would have given to this application of his writings: yes, of course, understanding Christianity is easy--almost as "easy" as infinite resignation, continual suffering, and total guilt, and these are only the first stage. Yes, of course, the "how" of the Christian way of life is accessible to all--have not the martyrs shown us the way?

Evidently there are some considerable differences among the figures which have been discussed in this chapter to illustrate dispositional treatments of religious faith.

(1) Whereas Braithwaite and Schmidt are content to analyze religion in terms of a "how" or "way of life," Nielsen argues that the "what" is indissolubly connected to the "how."

(2) Nielsen maintains that the "how" of religious life is either the same as that of secular man or accessible to the latter with very little trouble. Schmidt is readier than Nielsen to speak of a plurality of valid "ways of life,"[73] but in the end he does not think that any of the present-day religious stories are compatible with the scientific world view which we must all share, and the religion he recommends is a modified one which consists, for example, of stories and myths invented to encourage the development of the virtues of objective scientific research.[74] Braithwaite can be interpreted in either way on this point. His

---

by God talk. If the non-believer knows what it is to make a value-judgment and if he can make the usual empirical discriminations and if he is willing to or has in the past engaged in religious activities (carried out the appropriate operations), I do not see why he could not fully understand God talk." *Ibid.*, p. 129.

[72]*Ibid.* "Kierkegaard argues that Christ says that anyone can so understand, ... 'if anyone will follow my teaching, i.e., live according to it, i.e., act according to it, he shall see, etc.' Søren Kierkegaard, *Journals* (A. Dru translator) (New York: 1959), p. 185." (Abridged Edition.)

[73]*Religious Knowledge*, e.g., Chapter One, "A Look at Religions."

[74]*Ibid.*, Chapter Nine.

characteristic phrase "agapeistic way of life" suggests that there may be genuinely alternative ways of life, but he objects vehemently to the notion that there might be a peculiar logic of Christianity.[75] The Climacus writings, of course, are unequivocal here, and with the slogan "Subjectivity is untruth" announce that the Christian "how" is a distinctive one.

5. Conclusion

In this chapter we have explored some of the recent attempts to use dispositional concepts in speaking of religious faith. The relationship of our discussion to the previous chapter on Climacus is fairly close. The categories of the "how" and the "what" which he uses mark distinctions very similar to those of "knowing how" and "knowing that" which are employed by Schmidt. Yet the overall result of the juxtaposition of Climacus with the contemporary company is not to make them look more alike but rather to give a more emphatic sense of their dissimilarity. A chart can be constructed which will accommodate them all, but a good deal of pushing and shoving is necessary to fill the various cubicles and thus to keep Braithwaite, Schmidt, and Nielsen from collapsing into a common position (a universal, secularized morality of science, perhaps). And as these three pull together, Kierkegaard's Climacus is put into a more distinctive position than we had realized before.

In fact, the overall effect of placing Climacus beside the other three philosophers is to bring out more sharply the contrasts between them.

(1) The richness and detail of Climacus' description of faith is set off sharply from the rather vague terms the others employ. For Climacus there is nothing routine, nothing to be taken for granted about the "know how" of the way of faith. The "how" is not part of the standard equipment for the gentleman of the nineteenth century (or the twentieth, or any other). All "knowing how" requires training in some manner and degree, but so extraordinarily difficult to achieve is the capacity in this

---

[75]"An Empiricist's View of the Nature of Religious Belief," *Christian Ethics*, p. 94.

case that one wonders whether *anyone* can acquire it.[76] Braithwaite's man who hears the story of the Good Samaritan, and Nielsen's philosopher who performs certain religious practices, have not only not passed through Climacus' "existential training school"--they have not much more than entered the door.

(2) Climacus' isolation from other philosophers who use a dispositional analysis on the religious "how" is further heightened by certain distinctive terminology which he proposes for speaking about faith and knowledge.

A feature of the concept of knowledge which is brought out by the "knowing how"/"knowing that" analysis is that there are cases of knowledge to which the terms "true" and "false" do not easily apply. A "know how" is not "true" in any colloquial sense. Powell[77] uses this fact to argue that the concept of knowledge should be restricted to that area in which truth and falsity may be judged. Climacus takes in effect the opposite route, proposing that the concept of truth also be applied to a "know how." But lest there should be any confusion between the truth of "knowledge that" and the truth of "knowledge how" he calls the former "objective truth" and the latter "subjective truth."

Climacus' radicality does not consist in the fact that he makes a proposal about the use of "true," but in the unusualness of the proposal he makes. The ordinary usage of "true" is extremely flexible, and philosophers such as Powell have not been averse to restricting its ambiguity, either for the sake of neatness of terminology or to take advantage of the status bestowed on a judgment by that honorific word. Climacus, to prevent anyone from slighting the "how," marks it off as emphatically as possible with the expression "Subjectivity is truth."

(3) Climacus' redrawing of the boundaries of knowledge and truth is matched by a recognition of fine distinctions within those concepts. There are, he finds, kinds of "how"--aesthetic, ethical, and religious--and different ways in which a "what" may be related to a "how." Climacus need not be surprised, then,

---

[76] See *supra*, Chapter Two, B. Indeed, Kierkegaard in his later writing becomes increasingly dubious about whether the passion which is the precondition for Christianity any longer exists. See, e.g., XI^1 A 126 n.d. 1854.

[77] *Knowledge of Actions*, pp. 23-24; cf. *supra*, footnote 14.

when he finds that the "know how" in Christianity differs from that in ethics or aesthetics, in that Christianity requires certain preliminary communication of information.[78]

On the other hand, the application which Braithwaite, Schmidt, and Nielsen make of tools such as the disposition and "knowing how" concepts is a desultory, superficial, and rather unimpressive one. It is of interest chiefly as a contemporary suggestion for balancing other ways of doing philosophy of religion which restrict themselves primarily to the "what." But the framework from which these three operate is in fact built with the cognitive-conative-emotive divisions of the faculty psychology which is Ryle's primary target, and for the most part they merely provide new labels for old wares. Were it not for the anachronism one would be tempted to say that, of the philosophers of religion treated in this chapter, the only one who has taken the trouble to probe thoroughly into the implications of Ryle's distinction antedated his "teacher" by somewhat over one hundred years.

---

[78]Cf. Kierkegaard's comments, *supra*, Chapter Two, footnote 37.

CHAPTER FOUR

FAITH AND UNDERSTANDING: A CONTEMPORARY DEBATE

Introduction: The difference between the present and the previous chapter lies in the methods of the philosophers of religion who are discussed. Perhaps if Braithwaite, Schmidt, and Nielsen had turned out to be followers of Ryle, as the thrust of the previous chapter initially suggested, the chapter division here would have been superfluous and even misleading; but as it is, a bold, wide boundary line is required. For the effect of explicating Braithwaite and the others against a Rylean background is not to show the continuity with his work, but to heighten the sense of discontinuity.

The methodology which is employed by the men to be discussed next, however, is by no means simply a Rylean one, and frequently it is set forth vehemently in opposition to his views.[1] Far more influential than any other philosopher has been the work of Ludwig Wittgenstein, particularly in the *Philosophical Investigations*, *Remarks*, *Zettel*, and his unpublished lectures on philosophical psychology.

The question around which the debate revolves has already been foreshadowed in the discussion of Braithwaite, Schmidt, and Nielsen, through their treatment of the religious dispositions or "how." Is the "how" of the religious (and specifically the Christian) life part of a *general* "way of life" of modern, rational men, with a few archaic elements thrown in; or is there a *distinctive* "how" for the religious life? The overall answer of Braithwaite and his group is that the religious "how" is or ought to be considered as part of a general "way of life" established by scientific method and utilitarian morality. Moreover, what Kierkegaard said holds true here: if the "how" is given the "what" is also given. Thus it should not be surprising that when Braithwaite and the others play down the distinctiveness of the Christian "how" they also show little interest in a distinctively Christian "what."

---

[1]This opposition was, of course, also present among the men discussed in Chapter One, for example in the sections dealing with Bedford and Peters.

The answers of the men discussed in the present chapter line up on both sides of the question. It is of course understandable that to use one issue as the touchstone of the views of a number of men will result in a good deal of oversimplification, but we shall attempt to indicate where further refinement in distinctions would be appropriate.

The arrangement of the material of the debate is in the main chronological, although not so strictly as to make it simply a chronicle of the developments.

(1) Part One states the position of those who defend the view that there is a distinctive religious "how" (a position dubbed for convenience "linguistic pluralism"), as that view was presented up until 1962. The "pluralists" are critical of the roots of the position advocated by Braithwaite, and in this sense follow logically, although not entirely chronologically, upon the material discussed in the last chapter.

(2) Part Two takes up the "monistic" critique of linguistic pluralism in the philosophy of religion. Alasdair MacIntyre's article, "Is Understanding Religion Compatible with Believing?" (1962), is used to represent the stance of the critics up to the present.

(3) Part Three discusses the rejoinder to MacIntyre by Peter Winch in "Understanding a Primitive Society" (1964), together with others who represent the pluralistic position.

Following this brief account of the sides of the debate attention will be centered on issues which have been raised concerning ways of understanding alien traditions and concerning the possibility of rejecting religious belief.

A. The "Linguistic Pluralists" and Religious Belief

The expression "linguistic pluralism" is used here to identify a view of language in philosophy which allows for basic discontinuities among kinds of linguistic usages.[2] As opposed

---

[2] This expression is borrowed from Frankena's chapter in *Language, Thought, and Culture*, ed. Henle (Ann Arbor, 1965), p. 122. Frankena's exposition is more complex than what is adopted here. He speaks of "linguistic dualists" (Ogden and Richards, positivists) who divide language into two functions: "(1) the scientific, descriptive, representative, referential, (cont...)

to philosophical theories of language which separate all language uses into cognitive, emotive, and ethical types, these philosophers insist that there is a variety of distinguishable linguistic uses as great as the variety of human interests and actions. The pluralistic theory as applied to philosophical theology suggests that religion is misconceived if it is viewed, for example, as an indirect effort to account for the phenomena studied by physical science, or as an attractive dressing for ethical injunctions. Rather, religion includes a number of different modes of life, each of which has its own proper criteria for sense and nonsense and for correctness and incorrectness. In his book *The Idea of a Social Science*, Peter Winch gives a statement which aptly summarizes the pluralistic position:

> Criteria of logic are not a direct gift of God, but arise out of, and are only intelligible in the context of, ways of living or modes of social life. It follows that one cannot apply criteria of logic to modes of social life as such. For instance, science is one such mode and religion is another; and each has criteria of intelligibility peculiar to itself. So within science or religion actions can be logical or illogical: in science, for example, it would be illogical to refuse to be bound by the results of a properly carried out experiment; in religion it would be illogical to suppose that one could pit one's own strength against God's; and so on. But we cannot sensibly say that either the practice of science itself or that of religion is either illogical or logical; both are non-logical. (This is, of course, an over-simplification, in that it does not allow for the overlapping character of different modes of social life. Somebody might, for instance, have religious reasons for devoting his life to science. But I do not think that this affects the substance of what I want to say, though it would make its precise expression in detail more complicated.)[3]

In this particular quotation Winch gives the impression that there is a fairly small group of such sets of "criteria of intelligibility"--a logic of science, for example, and a logic of religion. In the rest of the book, however, it becomes clear

---

denotive, cognitive, etc., kind of meaning or use, and (2) the emotive, expressive, non-cognitive, etc., kind of meaning or use." He opposes to dualism both "linguistic pluralism" and a kind of "linguistic monism."

[3]*The Idea of a Social Science and its Relation to Philosophy* (London, 1958), pp. 100-01. The terms "logical," "illogical" and "non-logical" are taken from Pareto, the anthropologist whom Winch is criticizing in this passage.

that he is interested also in a great many other and subtler differences among the different modes of social activity and their distinctive criteria. He is particularly concerned to show that where the modes of society are not shared (e.g., between different cultures, especially with respect to matters such as religion) neither are the criteria of intelligibility; and that therefore there is a sense in which it is impossible for the non-participant in a culture fully to understand and evaluate the forms of social activity within it.

This thesis, that there is a variety of ways of understanding, as many as there are "ways of life," has been stated also by a number of other authors who touch on topics in the philosophy of religion, and the principles inherent in the notion have been applied in several ways.

(1) A characteristic application has been in the treatment of the so-called problem of the existence of God. Whatever sort of problem this may be, these men say, it is not a religious one. The existence of God is not a topic of debate *within* normal religious discourse, but only becomes a "problem" when that whole mode of social activity which is loosely bound up with the concept of God is called into question. There are "criteria of intelligibility" for the religious form of activity within which the concept of God performs an essential role. This concept therefore is religiously intelligible and not a conceptual problem at all in this context. If there are other (perhaps overlapping) modes of life with other criteria of intelligibility within which this concept of God also occurs, then this concept may be a problem conceptually; otherwise not.[4]

---

[4]"The assertion that God existed would have the ... function of being a profession of religious belief (not a vestigial explanation of what the belief was about). Outside of such a context, God's existence could not without confusion be denied any more than it could be asserted." R. F. Holland, "Modern Philosophers Consider Religion: A Reply," *Australasian Journal of Philosophy*, XXXVI (December, 1958), p. 209. In an earlier article Holland argues that the introduction of a special existent, God, might hurt the religious "how": "It might assist in the degeneration of worship into a species of opportunism." "Religious Discourse and Theological Discourse," *ibid.*, XXXIV (December, 1956), p. 163. Holland's point in the earlier article reminds one of "Religiousness A" as Kierkegaard conceives it; cf. *supra* in this essay, Chapter Two, C, 1.

(2) A development of the thesis along similar lines is made by Norman Malcolm in his well-known defense of a version of the ontological argument. He proposes that the concept of God should be understood in connection with "the human phenomena that lie behind it," such as "that human phenomenon of an unbearably heavy conscience."[5] There is a depth, Malcolm thinks, at which the ontological argument can be understood by anyone as a valid logical deduction. For a fuller understanding of the argument, however, it is necessary to see it against the background of the "how" within which the concept of God functions, and for such an understanding a participant's acquaintance with the "form of life" is required.

> At a deeper level, I suspect that the argument can be thoroughly understood only by one who has a view of that human "form of life" that gives rise to the idea of an infinitely great being, who views it from the *inside* not just from the outside and who has, therefore, at least some inclination to *partake* in that religious form of life. This inclination, in Kierkegaard's words, is "from the emotions."[6]

(3) With the denial that there are general criteria for all realms of discourse goes also a repudiation of the contention that ethical criteria can judge the appropriateness of religious concepts. Religious and moral concepts are indeed interrelated, but not in such a simple way. There is no universal ethical "how" by which all ethical and religious truth can be evaluated. Instead, we should speak, suggests Alasdair MacIntyre, of "alternative moralities,"[7] each of them intelligible though not each of them for that reason correct. In some of these moralities, though not in all, religious concepts are internally related to ethical ones.

---

[5] "Anselm's Ontological Arguments," *Religion and Understanding*, ed. D. Z. Phillips (Oxford, 1967), p. 61.

[6] *Ibid*. Italics in original. A similar treatment is given to the cosmological argument by D. Z. Phillips in "From World to God?" *PASS*, XLI (1967), pp. 133-52.

[7] *Difficulties in Christian Belief* (London, 1959), pp. 107-08. The position is attacked by Kai Nielsen in "Morality and God: Some Questions for Mr. MacIntyre," *PQ*, XII (April, 1962), pp. 129-37.

(4) As with the criteria of intelligibility, so also with the sources of proof: they operate appropriately only within the "how" in which they have their home.

> ... religion as a whole lacks any justification. But this in no way reflects on the logical standing of religious beliefs. Of science and morals it can also be said that one can justify particular theories or prescriptions, but that one cannot justify science as a whole in non-scientific, or morals as a whole in non-moral, terms. Every field is defined by reference to certain ultimate criteria. That they are ultimate precludes going beyond them.[8]

There are proofs in religion but they occur *within* the locus of belief. There is no proof for Christianity as a whole, any more than there is proof for any other mode of social activity.

Summary: Insofar as there is any common position among these thinkers it is that there is a plurality of ways in which intelligibility, morality, and proof play a part in human activity and specifically in religious activity. The sense of the concepts of intelligibility and the rest varies because there are differences among the "ways of life" in which they are rooted, and there are no established ways of adjudicating these differences.

B. The "Linguistic Monists" and Religious Belief

If the first group is called "linguistic pluralists" their opponents in the debate may be called by analogy "linguistic monists." The label turns out to be somewhat too extreme, but if accompanied by the proper qualification it will serve. (The expression "linguistic pluralists" also needs to be qualified, as we shall see, since those men are not by any means holding a radical relativist position.) What the "monists" wish to hold is not the traditional monistic position that there is an overall Reason (perhaps, e.g., the methodology of physics) which judges all matters in every field. Instead, they would say,

---

[8] Alasdair MacIntyre, "The Logical Status of Religious Belief," *Metaphysical Beliefs* (London, 1957), p. 202. Cf. MacIntyre, *Difficulties*, pp. 84-85, 117. The *Metaphysical Beliefs* article comes under severe attack from Basil Mitchell in "The Justification of Religious Belief," *New Essays in Religious Language* (New York, 1969), pp. 178-97.
Cf. Norman Malcolm, "Is It a Religious Belief that 'God Exists'?" *Faith and the Philosophers*, ed. Hick (London, 1964), pp. 108-09.

while certain concepts are field-dependent, there are others, such as "rationality," "truth," and "intelligibility," which are common to all fields and according to which statements in every field may be judged. This is not far from the hallowed philosophical doctrine of the "transcendentals," which has been used to assert the presence of divinely established natural norms.[9] But in the current discussion the position has rather been used to attack the possibility of holding religious belief at all; for the Thomistic framework is reversed, and the paradigm cases of the monists' transcendentals are located not in the essence of God but in the consciousness of a postulated secular modern man, and by this latter standard the religious uses of the concepts are ruled out of court.

1. MacIntyre

The position which will now be discussed is set down by Alasdair MacIntyre in a symposium at Princeton in 1962. He poses the question of pluralism vs. monism in terms of a dilemma:

> Usually ... two people could not be said to share a concept unless they agreed in at least some central applications of it.... For to possess a concept is to be able to use it correctly--although it does not preclude mishandling it sometimes. It follows that unless I can be said to share your judgements at least to some degree I cannot be said to share your concepts.
>
> Yet skeptic and believer disagree *in toto* in their judgements on some religious matters; or so it seems. So how can they be in possession of the same concepts? If I am prepared to say *nothing* of what you will say about God or sin or salvation, how can my concepts of God, sin and salvation be the same as yours? And if they are not, how can we understand each other? ... So it seems that we do want to say that a common understanding of religious concepts by skeptics and by believers is both necessary and impossible. This dilemma constitutes my problem.[10]

---

[9] Norris Clarke, S. J., who is otherwise very critical of MacIntyre, picks up this point of common ground in his response to MacIntyre's Princeton paper. "It is Compatible!" *Faith and the Philosophers* (London, 1964), pp. 135-36.

[10] "Is Understanding Religion Compatible with Believing?" *Faith and the Philosophers* (London, 1964), pp. 115-16. Note that this article from the 1962 Princeton symposium (and also "God and the Theologians") marks a radical switch on MacIntyre's part, from the pluralistic to the monistic side of the debate.

That the concepts of the religious life are shared, then, is both necessary (or else the skeptic cannot be rejecting the same thing as the believer accepts) and impossible (or else both the skeptic and the believer would be sharing the same judgments and thus holding the same views).

The inference which MacIntyre draws from this dilemma is that Christianity is either *unintelligible*, since its concepts cannot be shared by secular modern man; or else they are *irrelevant* to this same modern man, since he shares them already, and by accepting the Christian terminology would only be adopting a more pictorial vocabulary for the way of life he has. Let us examine both sides of this dilemma, beginning with the latter horn.

(1) If Christian believers share their religious concepts with skeptics, then these concepts are expendable. Except for ritual practices Christians today behave much the same as everyone else in our society, and insofar as Christian apologists suggest benefits from living the Christian life their proposals become a testable empirical hypothesis of doubtful significance.[11] Hegel's program for extracting the secular truth from "religious husks" has been put into effect.[12] "Christians behave like everyone else but use a different vocabulary in characterizing their behavior, and so conceal their lack of distinctiveness."[13] The distinctively Christian forms of behavior of past ages and even of the Confessing Church under Hitler are no longer relevant and have no clear sense in the current social situation.[14] And so, MacIntyre concludes, Christianity is a "form of belief which has lost the social context which once made it comprehensible. It is now too late to be medieval and it is too empty and too easy to be Kierkegaardian."[15]

(2) If Christian believers do not share their religious concepts with skeptics then these concepts are unintelligible.

---

[11]*Ibid.*, p. 131.

[12]*Ibid.*, p. 132.

[13]"God and the Theologians," *Encounter*, XXI (September, 1963), p. 9.

[14]"Is Understanding Religion Compatible with Believing?" p. 131; cf. "God and the Theologians" on Bonnhoefer, pp. 6-7.

[15]"Is Understanding Religion Compatible ... ?" p. 132.

MacIntyre recognizes that, contrary to what he says about the
sameness of the believers' and the skeptics' concepts, most contemporary religious writers have emphasized the "uniqueness of
religious utterance."[16] He cites Kierkegaard, Barth, and Marcel
as writers who show "an easy toleration for contradiction and
incoherence"[17] in their attempts to show the distinctiveness of
Christian concepts. But the "logical invulnerability" which
their efforts win for Christianity is only won, he maintains, at
the cost of emptiness, the "emptiness" of an untestable empirical
hypothesis.[18] Apparently, just as the Christian "how" is replaced
by a secular morality, the Christian "what" is replaced by the
results of modern science.

2. MacIntyre vs. Evans-Pritchard and Winch

Understanding Alien Cultures: As an illustration of the
nature of the problem of sharing concepts in religion, MacIntyre
turns to an analogous problem in anthropology: how is it that
anthropologists manage, if they do, to understand alien cultures
whose concepts they do not share? MacIntyre treats three different solutions by classical anthropologists and relates each to a
parallel solution in the philosophy of religion, but by far the
major part of his discussion is devoted to the anthropologist
Evans-Pritchard and to his supposed philosophical counterpart,
Peter Winch.

MacIntyre identifies Evans-Pritchard and Winch as up-
holders of the position at the one horn of his dilemma, that

---

[16]*Ibid.*, p. 130.

[17]*Ibid.*

[18]That the emptiness of which he speaks is that of an empty
empirical hypothesis comes out in the preceding argumentation,
which is directed against views like those of Crombie and Hick.
But the matter is an important one, far too critical to his argument to be brought up late and indirectly in his article. For
when all is said and done it is this point which provides MacIntyre with the "criteria of intelligibility" and coherence with
which he criticizes Kierkegaard, Barth, Marcel, and his own
previous views.
      A similar critique about the same time was made by Kai
Nielsen in "Can Faith Validate God-Talk?" *New Theology No. 1*, ed.
Marty and Peerman (New York, 1964), pp. 131-49. But in Nielsen
the verificationist strand is explicit and insistent, and no
serious attempt is made to deal with the pluralist position on
its own terms, and consequently this article belongs more in the
previous chapter than in this one.

where religious concepts are not shared they are intelligible to the participants but cannot be understood in any way by the non-participating observer. According to MacIntyre, Evans-Pritchard restricts himself to showing that the practices of the Nuer and the Azande people are intelligible and "have a point" for the participants,[19] and only allows these practices to be criticized on the basis of inherent criteria.[20] And this conclusion, thinks MacIntyre, is just what Winch also reaches when he sets up modes of social activity as autonomous entities.

Against Evans-Pritchard and Winch, MacIntyre brings a number of objections:

(1) The criteria for a practice cannot be inherent in the practice itself, or self-criticism of the criteria would not be possible.[21] Criteria change when, in a new social context, practices which were once intelligible lose their point.[22]

(2) A practice which is rule-governed and is thought to be intelligible by the participants in one culture may prove on the basis of a "more sophisticated understanding" such as ours[23] to have been simply "incoherent,"[24] and hence to lack "sense,"[25] "point and purpose,"[26] and "intelligibility."[27]

(3) "But in detecting incoherence of this kind," MacIntyre insists at a later point in the article, "we have already invoked *our* standards."[28] This is an important point. For it is not just that incoherence may arise through changing social conditions and disrupt the previously perfectly coherent set of

---

[19] "Is Understanding Religion Compatible ... ?" p. 119.

[20] *Ibid.*, p. 121.

[21] *Ibid.*, p. 120.

[22] *Ibid.*, p. 123.

[23] *Ibid.*, p. 121.

[24] *Ibid.*, pp. 122, 126.

[25] *Ibid.*, p. 122.

[26] *Ibid.*, p. 123.

[27] *Ibid.*, pp. 122-23.

[28] *Ibid.*, p. 126. Italics in original.

criteria governing the practices in a society.[29] The interesting cases are those which are now *and have always been* internally incoherent, but "this internal incoherence does not appear as such to the members of the society or else does appear and is somehow made tolerable."[30]

Source of the Criteria for Evaluating Alien Standpoints: But where do we find the criteria which are not simply relative to the social conditions of the times but which are capable of judging whether the practices of our own society and those of others are now or have ever been internally coherent? Despite his insistence that the criteria of social practices change as social forms develop, MacIntyre has very little doubt where he can find criteria with which to judge other ways of life than his own. Although he suggests that interpretation of alien cultures should begin with their self-description,[31] when he goes about the business of interpreting other cultures this preliminary glance at the participant's understanding is very brief indeed. He knows what the point of Azande magic is--a kind of protoscience and technology is what it amounts to on his view--and it is falsifiable in principle even though perhaps not in fact.[32] There is no particular difficulty for us with our modern science to understand what the Azande are about; but they, lacking the categories of science and non-science, are simply not in a position to criticize their own practices in a rational (i.e., scientific) way. The same kind of falsification test by means of which he judges that Azande magic is internally incoherent is applied to the Christian notion of omnipotent benevolence; this, too, is an hypothesis which the outsider can grasp without difficulty. But that the Christian doctrine is an empirical hypothesis and thus easily accessible to the trained skeptic, MacIntyre does

---

[29] This case is also used, however; the third example, *ibid.*, p. 127, is of a concept embedded in a form of life which is no longer practiced.

[30] *Ibid.*, p. 126. The first and second cases, p. 127, are of this type.

[31] *Ibid.*, p. 126.

[32] "We know very well what would falsify it ..." *ibid.*, p. 121.

not for a moment doubt. He only wonders how it will be possible to dismiss such a vaguely formulated hypothesis conclusively.[33]

As it turns out, then, MacIntyre does preserve from total relativization one set of criteria: his own. Azande witchcraft and Christian doctrines are unlikely-looking candidates for testing by the experimental procedures he outlines; but since these procedures provide the only categories he has available in his scheme of things, these alien doctrines and practices must be cut to fit.

The Horns of MacIntyre's Dilemma: How does it stand with MacIntyre's dilemma? At close inspection the situation is not nearly as straightforward as it first seemed. Let us consider the horns in turn:

(1) The first horn is that, although Christian practices had a point for people in the medieval period, for example, people see no point in them now and therefore find them superfluous for their lives. MacIntyre backs up this statement with remarks about secularization. But an increase of secularization (a matter on which sociologists of religion will have to rule) would not in any way discredit religious beliefs, any more than the contrary social tendency would warrant them.[34] MacIntyre

---

[33] *Ibid.*, p. 130.

[34] Norris Clarke, S. J., notes that whether a given culture makes a belief easier or harder to hold cannot make that belief objectively more valid. "Otherwise the argument could all too easily be turned against its wielder: since the social context today makes it easier to be an atheist or agnostic, these convictions themselves could thereby be discredited as mere culture-bound attitudes which in turn will lose meaning and relevance as soon as the present social context changes. But this would obviously land us in a hopeless cultural relativism depriving all views of life equally of any truth-value at all." MacIntyre cannot be making such a claim, Clarke says, nor can he be stating simply the sociological observation that it is harder to believe Christianity now than formerly. What he must mean, then, is that Christian belief is a "purely human construction resulting from social needs or pressures peculiar only to certain cultural contexts" and not "a response to an objective divine revelation." But such a position must deal with the fact that Christianity has existed in many social contexts and cultures, and is held by many outstanding scholars and scientists today. MacIntyre, however, does not even begin to bring forth evidence to counter this obvious difficulty for his claim. ("A Further Critique of MacIntyre's Thesis," *Faith and the Philosophers*, ed. Hick [London, 1964], pp. 147-48.) (cont...)

can preserve his thesis that the intelligibility of beliefs is dependent upon the existence of a certain shared social context (a point on which he and Winch are agreed), but if he tries to go beyond this he commits himself to a cultural relativism which undermines his own statements.

(2) The second horn appeals not to current secular morality but to experimental methods which he takes to be characteristic of contemporary culture. At this point MacIntyre forgets what he had said regarding the fact that the intelligibility of a set of beliefs is dependent upon its social milieu. The Azande and the Christians have their beliefs, which do not look like the experimental results of physics or meteorology or anything of that sort. But that is what MacIntyre calls them nevertheless. In fact, he thinks it is obvious that they are disguised scientific hypotheses, whatever their proponents may say, since that is the only way they can be intelligible to him.

Conclusion: The result of MacIntyre's placing of the appeal to contemporary morality and the appeal to experimental

---

An answer to this sort of challenge is provided by MacIntyre's 1964 Riddell Lectures (published as *Secularization and Moral Change* [Oxford, 1967]), in which he argues (p. 66) that Christianity includes a claim about "its necessary relevance to the forms of social life and its ability to give a meaning to secular social life in every kind of circumstance"; but surveys and studies show a decrease in church membership and activity in England and especially among the working class, and contemporary theologians have been unable to successfully interpret the Christian religion so that it would be at home in the modern world.
Some of the difficulties with MacIntyre's presentation are that:
(1) Christianity does not claim that belief will be easy, nor that it will be equally easy for all cultures and times; indeed, the apocalyptic tradition warns that in the last times belief will be impossible save by a miracle;
(2) MacIntyre's contention that Christianity has difficulty with the modern secular temper as such is weakened by the problem of defining any such temper;
(3) Such a sweeping claim should be based on a broader study than one limited to recent English history; MacIntyre gets uneasy even when discussing contemporary America, and hardly brings up other cultures or other times;
(4) He makes his critique of contemporary theology too easy for himself by devoting much attention to J. A. T. Robinson and using him as the lead into other theologians;
(5) It is not clear whether MacIntyre is prepared to reconsider his opinion of the truth of Christianity should there in the future be an increase rather than a decline in the popularity of Christianity among the English working class.

methods in parallel is to confuse the two. For instead of working together the two horns are logically conflicting: contemporary morality may indeed be relative, but then it constitutes no universal standard; whereas experimental methods do set a standard for certain sorts of inquiries (though their applications may be more culturally relative than MacIntyre allows), but they set no standards for morality. In fact, MacIntyre's relativizing of morality to a social context raises questions whether he is not bound to do the same for the particular view of the Western science he puts forward as the standard for all knowledge, and his absolutizing of the procedures of hypothesis and experiment makes one wonder whether he intends his relativism to apply only to other cultures and viewpoints and not to his own. The horns of the dilemma with which MacIntyre confronts the reader belong to two different beasts which do not get along well with each other; and while each of the beasts (unicorns perhaps) is formidable in his own right the logic of the situation suggests that no one will have to face them both at once.

3. The Case for Linguistic Monism

MacIntyre's attack on pluralism has a directness which his position in general lacks. The pluralists, and Winch in particular, he impales on the second horn of his dilemma, that is, they are accused of a radical relativism. In his standpoint he is joined by a number of others, who oppose the tendency they see in the pluralists toward a "compartmentalization of the forms of life,"[35] and a denial of the "human solidarity."[36] Indeed one writer, after accusing Winch of "onto-linguistic conservatism" and "neo-neo-Kantianism,"[37] suggests that Winch

---

[35] Nielsen, "On Believing that God Exists," *Southern Journal of Philosophy*, V (Fall, 1967), p. 170.

[36] Antony Flew, *God and Philosophy* (New York, 1966), p. 9. He is opposing Barth's thesis that "Belief cannot argue with unbelief: it can only preach to it!" Flew writes: "To concede such a claim would be to despair not only of reason but of human solidarity. It would be to accept a sort of religious racism; in which the saved and the damned are, at least in this most crucial respect, different kinds of creatures. It would be to recognize a cold war of the mind; in which there can be no room for genuine and fruitful dialogue between the enlightened and the unenlightened."

[37] D. B. Bell, "The Idea of a Social Science," *PASS*, XLI (1967), pp. 121-22.

> ... holds that the logical structures revealed by
> the sort of close ethnographic and cultural analysis
> typified by Evans-Pritchard's Azande witchcraft,
> constitute a synthetic *a priori* set of truths....
> Once baptize the Azande and Nuer view of their worlds
> with epistemological characteristics akin to those
> possessed by the Kantian categories, then reality
> (in this instance social reality) *must* conform to
> the ideas of the participants.[38]

If this is what Winch and company are holding then one can see how theories about general categories of rationality might be called in to salvage the shattered unity of the human race.[39]

---

[38] *Ibid.*, pp. 124-25.

[39] The critics of pluralism are not limited to non-Christians. In addition to Norris Clarke, S. J., (see *supra*, footnote 9), the chairman of the 1962 Princeton conference, John Hick, devotes a large part of his retrospective article on the conference to a critique of those whom he called "autonomists." His own position is that "Our reality terms--'real', 'exists', 'fact'--are modeled upon the kind of reality exhibited by the material world" (p. 246); and that they apply analogically to God, the difference in the sense of these terms arising out of the difference in the objects of cognition.
    Although Clarke and Hick take positions which remind one of Thomism, the general stance of the critics of pluralism is a verificationism which is close to or identical with the cognitive-conative-emotive split which was discussed in the previous chapter. MacIntyre has been used here as example, since he comes the closest of any to attempting to meet the pluralists on their own ground. Another major statement of monism in the philosophy of religion is "Wittgensteinian Fideism" by Kai Nielsen, *Philosophy*, XLII (July, 1967), pp. 191-209, which is an attack upon both Winch's "Understanding a Primitive Society" (see immediately *infra*) and upon a review by G. E. Hughes of Martin's *Religious Belief* in *Australasian Journal of Philosophy*, XL (August, 1962). Nielsen argues that both men fail to recognize the unity of language (p. 201) and to see the "overall universe of discourse of which religious discourse is a part" (p. 207).
    Nielsen's article suffers from a number of defects which derive from a confusion over what it is trying to do. It purports to be a critique of a large number of articles which represent "fideism," Nielsen's term for pluralism. But the ten articles and books he cites do not by any means form even the loosest sort of position, and some of the articles (e.g., those by Peter Geach and Robert Coburn) do not fit there at all. Some of his terminology seems to have been influenced by MacIntyre's paper, which he does not cite. This is particularly true of the constantly repeated term "coherent," which has a special sense for MacIntyre with his views on culture and language, but which becomes simply a slogan term for Nielsen. Like MacIntyre, Nielsen rests his positive case on an appeal to the verification principle (cf. footnote 18 *supra*), in the sense that there is a univocal "fact-stating" type of discourse which operates according to the verification principle and which must also work (cont...)

On the monists' account all the effort by the linguistic pluralists is quite wasted. There is no particular difficulty in grasping concepts which one does not share. Any fluent speaker of a language should be able to understand religious discourse.[40] Far from the Christian "how" being a task of extraordinary rigor it is something which the dullest skeptic can grasp and dismiss. It is, MacIntyre says, "too empty and too easy to be Kierkegaardian" any more.[41]

C. Third Phase: The Response of the "Pluralists"

1. Winch's Response to MacIntyre

MacIntyre's Misunderstandings: The reaction of the pluralists to the objections from MacIntyre and his group is to deny any wish to defend the position the monists attack. No one rushes to the battlements to fight for the notion that religion or any other mode of social activity cannot be understood *ab externo*, and there are no champions for "neo-neo-Kantianism" or "compartmentalization of the forms of life."

MacIntyre's strictures on Winch meet with an especially blank reception. In an article entitled "Understanding a Primitive Society"[42] Winch argues convincingly that MacIntyre's criticisms are based on persistent misunderstandings of several crucial points:

(1) Contrary to MacIntyre's criticism, Winch does recognize that concepts and the criteria for their use change with different social patterns, and in fact a great deal of his argument is based on this very factor.[43] In his later article on Winch MacIntyre repeats the point without retracting or defending

---

in religious discourse if religion is to be taken seriously. Cf. Nielsen's articles on the verification debate in theology, "Eschatological Verification" and "God and Verification Again," *Canadian Journal of Theology*, IX (1963, No. 4), pp. 271-81, and XI, No. 2 (1965), pp. 135-41.

[40]Nielsen, "Wittgensteinian Fideism," p. 207.

[41]MacIntyre, "Is Understanding Religion Compatible ... ?" p. 132.

[42]Peter Winch, "Understanding a Primitive Society" (1964), *Religion and Understanding*, ed. Phillips (Oxford, 1967), pp. 9-42.

[43]*Ibid.*, p. 32.

it; but even Bell, who otherwise vehemently opposes Winch and all his works and ways, grants that MacIntyre is mistaken here.[44]

(2) Moreover, Winch does *not* propose, in fact he explicitly denies,[45] that only the participants of a society have the categories to understand it, and that therefore a social scientist cannot profitably use alien categories in order to describe a culture different from his own.[46] Winch does insist that there are some senses of "understanding" in which it is impossible for an outsider to understand who does not share the practices within which the criteria are embedded. He cites as an example here an unpublished paper of Anscombe that there are certain activities such as mathematics which, unlike acrobatics, "cannot be understood by an observer unless he himself possesses the ability to perform the activities in question."[47] Any description of activities like arithmetic which is not based on arithmetical practices is bound to seem pointless and arbitrary. But this sort of point, which Winch makes variously throughout the book, does not in any way preclude that there are ways of understanding and activities which are open to both the participant and the trained observer; and in fact Winch points out examples of this kind of study, such as the work of Evans-Pritchard.

Sharing Concepts: To MacIntyre's dilemma Winch replies by in effect escaping between the horns and denying the simple disjunction on which the dilemma is based. It is not just a matter of sharing a concept or not, but of sharing the concept in various ways and degrees, for various purposes. The broad philosophical concepts such as intelligibility, truth, rationality, and coherence are no different in this respect from other concepts. In fact these "transcendentals," far from being the easiest concepts to pin down, are among the most shifting and elusive, and consequently it is especially important in these cases to pay attention to the "how" in which they function in a particular case.

---

[44] MacIntyre, "The Idea of a Social Science," *PASS*, XLI (1967), p. 112; Bell, *ibid.*, pp. 116-17.

[45] *The Idea of a Social Science*, p. 89.

[46] This is the conclusion MacIntyre draws about Winch's standpoint; "Is Understanding Religion Compatible ... ?" p. 120.

[47] Winch, *The Idea of a Social Science*, p. 109.

Winch makes this point in the volume which MacIntyre criticizes, but it goes unnoticed by his critic. There are, Winch says, various kinds of understanding. The concept of intelligibility is "systematically ambiguous"; that is, "its sense varies systematically through functioning in different systematic structures according to the particular context in which it is being used."[48] The kind of intelligibility a concept has, and thus the kind of understanding it permits, is embedded in the social structures in which the concept has its home.

2. Systematically Ambiguous Concepts

What is true of the concept of intelligibility is true, according to Winch and the other pluralists, of the other pivotal concepts as well. As there are different ways of being intelligible, so there are different criteria for making sense, being correct, and being coherent or avoiding contradiction.[49] Donald Hudson, in a reply to Nielsen's "Wittgensteinian Fideism" article, points out that Nielsen's case rests on finding in concepts such as "real" and "reasonable" just those aspects which agree with his own outlook. Hudson argues, like Winch, that these concepts cannot be staked out in such a simplistic way; they are, he says, "systematically elusive," "systematically indefinable."[50]

---

[48] *Ibid.*, p. 18; cf. pp. 22-24. The expression derives from Gilbert Ryle's article by that title, reprinted in *Logic and Language*, First Series (New York, 1965), pp. 13-39.

[49] Winch, "Understanding a Primitive Society," pp. 9, 22, 23, 31; on "fact" cf. Winch, "Nature and Convention," *PAS*, LX (1959-60), pp. 236-38.

[50] "On Two Points Against Wittgensteinian Fideism," *Philosophy*, XLIII (July, 1968), pp. 272-73. In his book *Ludwig Wittgenstein: The Bearing of His Philosophy Upon Religious Belief* (Richmond, Va., 1968) Hudson cites Wittgenstein's *Lectures and Conversations* (pp. 57-58) on "reasonableness" and religious belief:

"Here we have people who treat this evidence in a different way. They base things on evidence which taken in one way would seem exceedingly flimsey. They base enormous things on this evidence. Am I to say they are unreasonable? I wouldn't call them unreasonable.
"I would say, they are certainly not *reasonable*, that's obvious.
"'Unreasonable' implies, with everyone, rebuke.
"I want to say: they don't treat this as a matter of reasonability.
"Anyone who reads the Epistles will find it said: not only that it is not reasonable, but that it is folly. (cont...)

Similarly, in a chapter entitled "Faith, Scepticism and Religious Understanding," D. Z. Phillips argues against the attempt to ask religious language to conform to criteria of meaningfulness which are alien to it.

> They say that religion must be rational if it is to be intelligible. Certainly, the distinction between the rational and the irrational must be central in any account one gives of meaning. But this is not to say that there is a paradigm of rationality to which all modes of discourse conform. A necessary prolegomenon to the philosophy of religion, then, is to show the diversity of criteria of rationality; to show that the distinction between the real and the unreal does not come to the same thing in every context.[51]

Efforts to make one paradigm of rationality operate in all cases can only distort the subtle differences among conceptual contexts.

3. Problems in the Pluralistic Position

But can such "systematically ambiguous" concepts preserve a unity so that modes of life do not dissolve into unintelligible bits? There are two aspects of this question:

(1) There is the problem whether treating language in terms of "language games," each with separate rules, does not destroy the unity of language and of human activity. Rush Rhees in a discussion of Wittgenstein draws attention to such a danger in handling "language games" as isolated units. Rather, he says, the use of any concept in a particular case depends to some degree on its use in other related but different language games.[52] Winch, commenting on this remark, emphasizes it:

> Language games are played by men who have lives to live--lives involving a wide variety of different

---

"Not only is it not reasonable, but it doesn't pretend to be."

Here we have the opposite but complementary proposal to that of Winch. Instead of speaking of ways of rationality of which religion is one, he speaks of ways of acting appropriately which are not "reasonable." Wittgenstein is here closer to the Kierkegaard of the *Postscript* than is Winch.

[51]"Faith, Scepticism and Religious Understanding," *Religion and Understanding* (Oxford, 1967), p. 68.

[52]"Wittgenstein's Builders," *Wittgenstein: The Man and His Philosophy*, ed. Fann (New York, 1967), pp. 251-64.

> interests, which have all kinds of different bearings
> on each other. Because of this, what a man says or
> does may make a difference not merely to the perfor-
> mance of the activity upon which he is at present
> engaged, but to his *life* and to the lives of other
> people. Whether a man sees point in what he is doing
> will then depend on whether he is able to see any
> unity in his multifarious interests, activities, and
> relations with other men; what sort of sense he sees
> in his life will depend on the nature of this unity.[53]

There is, then, a unity within a man's life and within the life of a group, which, although looser than the unity of a set of rules for a language game, lends a genuine cohesiveness to the whole.

(2) Is there also a generality for these concepts wider than the life of a man or a group? In a certain sense we may speak of a unity of the human race. In the 1964 article Winch discusses this unity of a man's life in society in terms of three common human concerns[54]--birth, death, and sexual relations-- which occur in all cultures, even though their place in different cultures may be very diverse.[55] But he also touches at several points on another, much more controversial thesis, which he develops in more detail in an earlier article,[56] that such a concept as truth may be inevitable for any human society. His argument is that "there could not be a human society in which truthfulness were not in general regarded as a virtue."[57] A person can manipulate his words to suit his ends on certain occasions but "not all, or even most, uses of language can be so regarded."[58] For if persons did not mutually commit themselves to keeping the rules of the language games they share, communication and social living would not be possible. A similar case can be made, he

---

[53]"Understanding a Primitive Society," pp. 36-37.

[54]*Ibid.*, p. 38: "certain fundamental notions."

[55]*Ibid.*, pp. 38-42.

[56]"Nature and Convention," *PAS*, LX (1959-60), pp. 231-52.

[57]*Ibid.*, p. 250.

[58]*Ibid.*, p. 249.

thinks, for the concept of integrity[59] and perhaps also for justice.[60]

This does not mean that, after all, one can now resurrect a single paradigm of truth, and with it one of rationality, intelligibility, and the rest, and with these standards judge the varied kinds of human activities in this and in other cultures.

> To say that the virtue of truthfulness must play some part in the life of any society is not to describe the peculiar part it plays in the life of a particular society.[61]

It does not, with MacIntyre, give us a license to demand that the standards of our particular culture be those to which any other society must conform or that the criteria of intelligibility and coherence of any given science, such as physics, be imposed on all other human activities. *Some* form of rationality, *some* form of intelligibility, *some* form of coherence will be there. But what form it will be we cannot dictate in advance; we must "look and see."

4. Passionate Disagreement

The Possibility of Disagreement Over Central Concepts: Part of MacIntyre's dilemma has not been discussed explicitly, because although it is a crucial point it is not one on which he dwells. If Christians and skeptics do not share the same concepts, he says, then how does it make sense for the one to reject what the other says?[62]

The remarks which were just cited by the pluralists suggest a response which could be given. Many concepts, they might say, are not possessed in an all-or-nothing, standardized form. Certainly concepts such as rationality, intelligibility, and coherence are not. Indeed, what would the standardized, complete possession of the concept of intelligibility be? But this does not mean that the concepts are totally ambiguous. There are many different ways and degrees of being intelligible and many paradigms for each way. Yet there are also commonalities, and

---

[59] *Ibid.*, pp. 250-51.

[60] *Ibid.*, p. 252.

[61] *Ibid.*, p. 250.

[62] "Is Understanding Religion Compatible ... ?" p. 116.

although the area on which all men agree may be small (and perhaps trivial) there is enough overlap in discussions even between highly disparate groups so that communication takes place to some extent. We ought to take this fact of communication for what it is, and for nothing more nor less--not for the deceptively appearing discord masking a full agreement on the basic concepts (so that, for instance, one would have to say that the Azande fully share MacIntyre's concept of intelligibility but are not aware of it), but for a *partial* sharing of the concepts which may (or may not) permit a *limited* understanding on both sides. Whether the conclusions of the Azande or any alien group are accepted or rejected will depend, then, on only partially shared concepts. And on topics such as witchcraft where the disputed concepts of rationality, intelligibility, and the like are so intimately involved, we would do well to be cautious in treating the acceptance or rejection as anything like that which takes place when concepts are more fully shared.

Passionate Acceptance or Rejection of Christianity: But beyond these very general remarks can we specify more definitely any sort of acceptance or rejection which may be involved in conversion or apostasy? Taking a hint from Kierkegaard's Climacus we can say some things about the change involved. Only two kinds of people understand Christianity, he says:

> ... those who with an infinite passionate interest in an eternal happiness base this their happiness upon their believing relationship to Christianity, and those who with an opposite passion, but in passion, reject it--the happy and unhappy lovers.[63]

Faith is a happy passion, offense an unhappy one; in neither case is a dispassionate attitude possible. The skeptic who is offended in Climacus' sense sees the "point" of Christianity from the inside, and for this very reason rejects Christianity vehemently as a threat to all his expectations and desires.

Of course Kierkegaard's is not the only possible concept of faith or of skepticism. In Kierkegaard's sense the "modern" man whom MacIntyre describes can be neither faithful nor skeptical, since that man fails to see the point of Christianity. But the concepts of passionate faith and of passionate skepticism

---

[63]*Postscript*, p. 51.

are nevertheless very much a part of the modern scene. D. Z. Phillips points to the figure of Camus' "rebel"--the man who shares the pathos of the Christian story but is repulsed by it and therefore struggles against it.[64] In a similar vein Kierkegaard writes that Feuerbach understands Christianity better than the systematizers;[65] for Feuerbach attacks it passionately, while they trivialize it by turning it into a matter of merely academic concern.

MacIntyre and Kierkegaard: There is certainly some arbitrariness in the conceptual distinctions which are in dispute between Kierkegaard and the monists. One *can* draw the boundary lines of faith as MacIntyre does, so that everyone is included who expresses or implies some preference for a creed, and draw the lines of skepticism so widely that anyone is a skeptic who fails to see the point of the belief--with the result that great numbers of people in England are listed as believers simply on the basis of their casual acceptance of some articles of faith, while these same people qualify as skeptics of Azande magic and innumerable other viewpoints even though they have never bothered to inquire what those viewpoints mean from the inside.

Nevertheless, although MacIntyre's usage is a possible one, a definite sharpening of the categories is achieved when one centers on some of the clear cases of faith and skepticism. For this reason Kierkegaard insists that the concepts of faith and skepticism be drawn narrowly: simply belonging to a folk church is not enough to make one faithful, except in a vague and misleading sense, and simply finding no use for a creed in one's own conceptual scheme will make one merely a tepid skeptic. To be a man of faith requires passion, and to be a man of doubt requires passion too. Skepticism, like faith, has its heroes and

---

[64]"Faith, Scepticism and Religious Understanding," p. 78: "He sees the story from the inside, but it is not a story which captivates him." He is the "unhappy lover" (p. 79). Cf. *Concept of Prayer* (London, 1965), p. 28, and "Philosophy, Theology, and the Reality of God," *PQ*, XIII (October, 1963), p. 350.

[65]X^2 A 163, p. 129. See Karl Löwith, *From Hegel to Nietzsche* (Garden City, N. Y., 1967), p. 357.

its martyrs, and again like faith it is betrayed when it is made easy and common.[66]

The passionate skeptic, the rebel, understands the Christian faith in a decisive way which another man with a merely academic interest in the topic does not. Does the rebel then fully share the Christian concepts? MacIntyre's either/or is as misleading here as elsewhere. Does the unhappy lover, the one who with passion rejects his loved one, understand fully the joys and sorrows which he will not share? Probably not, but there is no pat answer. The metaphor of the unhappy lover is a sketch of a kind of understanding which is more than that from a dispassionate interest and less than that from a whole-hearted commitment.

D. Conclusions and Correctives

1. The End of a Debate

The terms according to which the debate in this chapter is conducted are (1) that the question is whether a "pluralistic" or a "monistic" framework is superior for representing the logic of religious belief, and (2) that the tools used are those of contemporary analytical "philosophical psychology," particularly as that was practiced by Wittgenstein.

In the course of the exchanges it becomes clear that the monistic-pluralistic split is an oversimplified one. The monists fling charges of "relativism" and "fideism" at their opponents, and the pluralists reply that they are nothing of the kind. But neither position is as simple as the charges would suggest.

MacIntyre's 1962 article is an attempt to challenge on its own ground the use of Wittgensteinian motifs for a pluralistic stance. But in a more recent article[67] criticizing Winch he shifts his position on several crucial points, so that the two no longer are working from a common basis. The same movement

---

[66]Kierkegaard has in fact a lively and sympathetic interest in the "honest doubters," among whom he numbers the Greek skeptics and Descartes, because (as opposed to the Hegelians) they lived their doubt and did not try to overcome it by turning it into an abstraction. See *De Omnibus* appendix, pp. 181, 185-89.

[67]In "The Idea of a Social Science" (1967), p. 95, MacIntyre acknowledges that the conclusions he reaches in opposition to Winch are also contrary to his own prior position, as given for example in "A Mistake about Causality in Social Science," *Philosophy, Politics, and Society*, Second Series (Oxford, 1962), pp. 48-70.

can be seen still more clearly in Nielsen, whose interest in the methods of Wittgenstein and his followers has never been as apparent as MacIntyre's.[68]

The outcome of the debate, together with the publication of new Wittgenstein materials,[69] implies that a Wittgensteinian and Rylean methodology favors a "linguistic pluralism" also in the philosophy of religion. "Language games," "forms of life" and "systematically ambiguous expressions" are expressions which suggest a flexibility and variety in our concepts which undermine the monistic position. Further criticism of the pluralistic point of view must therefore take on not simply the applications of these philosophical tools to questions about religious belief but also the validity of the tools themselves.

2. Essentially Contested Concepts

W. B. Gallie: Beyond the fact that it shows that the pluralistic position concerning religious belief is favored by the framework of the "philosophical psychology" of Wittgenstein and Ryle, the debate also indicates a strength in the pluralistic position in its own right. To explore this result let us examine the status of the question concerning "systematically elusive" or "ambiguous" expressions in terms of a helpful terminology developed by W. B. Gallie in an article entitled "Essentially Contested Concepts."[70]

Gallie's thesis is that general concepts such as those which we have described in this chapter may be employed in

---

[68] Nielsen's earlier articles occasionally use Wittgensteinian expressions, as if they were part of an accepted *lingua franca*, and he is unsure whether Wittgenstein's statements have pluralistic implications; but in his "Wittgensteinian Fideism" article he hopes out loud that Wittgenstein would not have approved of what his followers have done. But the body of that article was written before the publication of Wittgenstein's *Lectures and Conversations*, and in his later articles he recognizes that his quarrel is not only with the disciples but with Wittgenstein as well and the way of doing philosophy which he represents. In "Wittgensteinian Fideism Again: A Reply to Hudson," *Philosophy*, XLIV (January, 1969), p. 65, footnote 3, he mentions that in his forthcoming *Quest for God* volume he will criticize Wittgenstein's statements about religious belief. (Cf. *supra*, footnote 50 of this chapter.)

[69] In addition to the *Lectures and Conversations*, these include his "Bemerkungen über Frazers *The Golden Bough*," *Synthese*, XVII (1967), pp. 233-53.

[70] *The Importance of Language*, ed. Max Black (Englewood Cliffs, N. J., 1962), pp. 121-46.

disputes "which are perfectly genuine: which although not resolvable by argument of any kind, are nevertheless sustained by perfectly respectable arguments and evidence."[71] These "essentially contested" concepts are persistently ambiguous, because they possess a number of different aspects which can legitimately be emphasized by the parties in a dispute concerning them. But they also have a unity, in that discussion of them makes appeal to some sort of exemplar or to a common tradition.[72]

The picture is of a number of groups of people competing for allegiance to the use of a particular interpretation of a concept which has a tradition or common exemplar. Gallie employs the whimsical example of a group of teams competing for a championship when they do not know just what the concept of a champion would mean in their game--whether it was judged by the speed of the attack, or the number of goals, or the complicated finesse of the play. Although there would never be a conclusive way of deciding who the champion was, there are reasons which can be

---

[71] *Ibid.*, p. 123.

[72] Gallie cites seven characteristics of such a concept:
(1) "It signifies or accredits some kind of valued achievement" (p. 125);
(2) It is "internally complex," that is, it has a number of different aspects, which can be emphasized and arranged differently by the various parties in a dispute (p. 125);
(3) It is initially ambiguous (3a, footnote p. 125); "the accredited achievement is *initially* variously describable"; "prior to experimentation there is nothing absurd or contradictory in any one of a number of possible rival descriptions of its total worth" (from 3, p. 125);
(4) It is "*persistently* vague" (from 4a, footnote p. 125); "The accredited achievement must be of a kind that admits of considerable modification in the light of changing circumstances; and such modification cannot be predicted in advance" (from 4, p. 125);
(5) "Each party recognizes the fact that its own use of it is contested by those of other parties" (p. 125);

In addition to these characteristics which guarantee that the concept shall be recognized as throughout ambiguous and contested, Gallie gives two which contribute to making it a unified concept:

(6) The achievement sought is derived in some way from an exemplar or prototype which is recognized by the disputants, or there is a common tradition to which they can and do appeal (pp. 128-29, 131);
(7) There is plausibility in the claim that "the continuous competition for acknowledgment as between the contestant users of the concept, enables the original exemplar's achievement to be sustained and/or developed in optimum fashion" (p. 131).

brought forward and appeals which can be made to a tradition. Thus, while their dispute over the championship concept presents no possibility of ultimate universal agreement, individual members may decide to switch teams because of reasons which have genuine logical force.[73]

"Essentially Contested Concepts" and the Monist-Pluralist Debate: What Gallie's framework and his discussion of examples ("the Christian life," "democracy," and "social justice") show is that the sharing of concepts is a much more complex matter than MacIntyre's either/or allows, even with the admission that concepts may be shared in various degrees. Gallie's appreciation of traditions, paradigms, and aspects allows us to separate out some of the distinctions which MacIntyre's dilemma, and the type of thinking it represents, tends to obscure.

For religious concepts may be shared in quite different ways:

(1) Where the disputed concepts come as part of a definite, identifiable tradition. This is the case with Gallie's favorite instance, "the Christian life," an obviously relevant example. Within the Christian tradition in any era there are—necessarily, Gallie thinks—a number of dissenting sects who fasten on differing aspects of a concept such as "the Christian life," and yet accept the same paradigm. The possibility of heresy will arise in the Christian tradition and, while it cannot be deduced *a priori*, nevertheless is rendered very likely by the very nature of the concept dealt with. Here there is no division between skeptics and believers, but between groups of believers who do not altogether share the same concepts and yet who can rationally disagree.[74]

---

[73]" ... what I am claiming is that a certain piece of evidence or argument put forward by one side in an apparently endless dispute can be recognized to have a definite logical force, even by those whom it entirely fails to win over or convert to the side in question; and that when this is the case, the conversion of a hitherto wavering opponent of the side in question can be seen to be *justifiable*--not simply expectable in the light of known relevant psychological or sociological laws-- given the waverer's previous state of information and given the grounds on which he previously supported one side and opposed the other." *Ibid.*, p. 140.

[74]*Ibid.*, pp. 132-33.

(2) Where the disputed concepts occur within the confines of a very broad, almost indefinable tradition. What this category would include would be cases in which the concepts were spoken of as part of "the Western tradition" or perhaps of "the modern world." There are archetypes and traditions which may be drawn upon even here, but they are often extremely elusive.[75] Where is the paradigmatic "modern man"? When MacIntyre appeals to "the modern world" he is using what is in this respect an essentially contested concept, although he uses the concept in his argument as if it were definite and even brings in sociological data. As Clarke points out,[76] MacIntyre does not deal seriously with the vast plurality of traditions and paradigms bidding for the allegiance of contemporary man.

(3) Where the disputed concepts lie outside a common tradition or prototype, but where a partially common tradition can perhaps be established by sympathetic contact. Winch[77] states that MacIntyre, by fixing the crucial concepts, does not allow for the possibility that, confronted with an unfamiliar way of thinking, we may decide to *expand* our own concepts and categories. A new "tradition" is then established even between people of different cultures and there is a certain limited understanding possible on the basis of this new common ground.

(4) Where the disputed concepts lie outside a common tradition, broad or narrow, and there is no way in which such a tradition can be even partially established. If this turns out to be the case, all one can do is to agree to disagree; but one must not give up too soon.

Conclusion: It would, of course, be possible to continue this list, but carrying it this far is sufficient for the purpose. MacIntyre's argument is that religious beliefs and practices can be dealt with by a scientific apparatus and that therefore the

---

[75] One of Gallie's examples fits in at this point better than in (1). He speaks of the concept of art as one which includes many quite distinct traditions and which lacks any obvious universal prototype. But he notes that in any intelligent discussion of the concept it is usually fairly easy to determine what artistic tradition forms the model for the concept. *Ibid.*, p. 133.

[76] "It is Compatible!" p. 141.

[77] "Understanding a Primitive Society," p. 37.

beliefs and practices cannot have a distinctively religious function. But when the categorial alternatives are multiplied indefinitely by making allowance for a plurality of overlapping sets of concepts to deal with the same matter together with shared traditions and paradigms, MacIntyre's dilemma is eliminated; and with its passing fades also another threat which he holds before us, of the inevitability, where concepts are appealed to by both skeptics and believers, of interminable and fruitless disputes.

3. The Concept of Passionate Faith

How does the discussion affect and how is it affected by Climacus' conception of faith as a "happy passion"?

(1) The sharp disjunction between "Subjectivity is truth" and "Subjectivity is untruth" may be modified somewhat, once one allows for the variety of ways in which concepts may be shared. Especially in the *Fragments*[78] the "new creature," whose subjectivity is untruth, is so marked off from his fellow creature who has not been offended by the Paradox, that one may wonder whether both of them belong to the same human race, even though we are assured that they do. Likewise in the *Postscript* two of the remarks, that the Paradox has no analogy[79] and that faith constitutes a breach with all thinking,[80] may easily arouse concern that faith may be cut off from unfaith altogether.

The loosening of the categories by pluralism renders such extreme measures in the *Fragments* and the *Postscript* unnecessary,[81]

---

[78]*Fragments*, p. 120.

[79]*Postscript*, p. 529.

[80]*Ibid.*, p. 513.

[81]This is not to say that the Climacus figure we find in the *Fragments* and the *Postscript* would necessarily welcome such a scheme as Gallie proposes. Since Climacus is suspicious lest faith be made "rational" and the way of "fear and trembling" replaced by a superhighway of congenial, erudite dialogue, he might not put much stock in Gallie's point (*supra*, footnote 72, #7) that the competition among the users of a concept is what sustains and develops that concept.

Perhaps the approach adopted by this essay, of selecting one figure in the Kierkegaardian "Literature" as the spokesman for a viewpoint, gets in the way here of a balanced evaluation of Kierkegaard's contribution. Taken as a whole his "Literature" provides a remarkable gallery of kinds of human subjectivity. He not only allows for, he insists upon, the diversity, (cont...)

except of course as Kierkegaard may have wanted to use the sharp dichotomy as a polemical device for a corrective of Hegelian thinking. The distinctiveness of faith and the absurdity of its categories to the outside can all be affirmed without making discussions between faith and unfaith impossible--nor, on the other hand, promising that the discussions will be any simpler or more profitable than the fruitless exchanges they often turn out to be.

(2) In turn, Kierkegaard can make a contribution toward modifying the discussion of religious belief in pluralistic terms, by his recognition of the place of a "what" along with the "how." Both the monists such as MacIntyre (and Braithwaite and Schmidt, who should be counted here) and the pluralists such as Malcolm, Winch, and Phillips, rest everything on the "how." Gallie also follows these lines when as an example of a Christian concept he picks out the "Christian life." Kierkegaard, on the other hand, has a place for the "what" along with the "how." Moreover, he has managed to do this without in the least detracting from the paramount importance of the "how," and in fact he gives an unsurpassed urgency to the "how" and to the extraordinary rigor it demands.[82] He provides very little indication of the way in which the two are related--logically, causally, or however--beyond affirming that if the "how" is given the "what" is also given, and allowing for a "fit" between the two.[83] But even

---

development, and overlapping character of these portraits; they are all part of "becoming a Christian." He surely would not want to have the view ascribed to him that there are only two kinds of subjectivity, faithful and unfaithful, which can never meet. The differences among the figures in his gallery cannot, it is true, be finally adjudicated by debate, and to think that they can may result in all sorts of absurdities; but the various figures can (and do, for example in *Either/Or* and the *Stages*) discuss coherently with each other.

On the basis of the diversity of categories in Kierkegaard's authorship, Phillips uses him as an example of pluralism: "So there are criteria of truth and falsity, right and wrong, depth and shallowness, within what Kierkegaard calls subjectivity. But these criteria belong to the realm of faith itself. The love of God is not based on the facts, but is itself the measure by which the Christian assesses the facts." ("Subjectivity and Religious Truth in Kierkegaard," *Sophia*, VII [July, 1968], p. 8.)

[82]Cf. *supra*, end of Chapter Three, pp. 89-91.

[83]Cf. *supra*, metaphor of the lovers, Chapter Two, pp. 57-58.

Conclusions and Correctives 123

these hints, elusive as they are, may be suggestive if they are developed within the context of a philosophy which allows for ambiguity and variety in the concept of knowledge,[84] instead of against the background of a rationalistic scheme.

(3) In addition to this contribution Kierkegaard also makes another, related one, which has made some impression on the debate, though perhaps not as much as it deserves.[85] It would be easy, with all the talk by Gallie about tradition, to make of the "Christian life" a set of folkways to be absorbed almost unconsciously from one's particular social grouping. Kierkegaard knew this view, as it was represented in the state church and as it had received new form in the movement of Grundtvig, but instead of lauding it he reserved for it some of his sharpest satirical barbs. He did not depreciate the importance of training and upbringing,[86] but he did insist that faith cannot be acquired by absorbing the rules for a way of life.[87] Faith is a passion, a passion with a character in some ways peculiar to itself; but it is like some other passions in that it seizes a man and will not let him go, at the same time as it summons him to develop his subjectivity in a certain distinctive way. Without the passion the rules lose their force; they have no point. The man who can cite the rules and detail the patterns

---

[84] Cf. *supra*, Chapter Three, pp. 70-76.

[85] Cf. Phillips, *supra*, footnote 64, p. 107.

[86] See, e.g., *Authority and Revelation* (New York, 1966), p. 164: "In order to express oneself Christianly there is required, besides the more universal language of the heart, also skill and schooling in the definition of Christian concepts, while at the same time it is of course assumed that the emotion is of a specific, qualitative sort, the Christian emotion."

[87] It is too much to say that Winch is not aware of this particular danger of making religion and other forms of social activity into games and ceremonies. When A. R. Louch accuses him of restricting himself to explicitly ruled behavior in the social sciences he rightly denies that this was any part of what he had set forth. (Louch, "The Very Idea of a Social Science," *Inquiry*, VI [Winter, 1963], pp. 273-86; Winch, "Mr. Louch's Idea of a Social Science," *Inquiry*, VII [Summer, 1964], pp. 202-08.) Nevertheless, it is true that Winch's exposition of human activity in terms of "language games" does lay him open to the misunderstanding that he is satisfied if he can cite the rules for the game, even if he does not see the game's point.

of behavior and their interconnections, but lacks the passion, has a kind of understanding (one which could be acquired by rote), but he has not grasped what is important and decisive in the concepts. Likewise, skepticism is a passion, which sees the point but vehemently rejects it. One should therefore not be surprised if faith and skepticism lose their point when made over into dispassionate formulae, for in the process of transfixing them to the specimen board the passion which is their life has been lost. The dispassionate understanding suffices for the *Dozent* and the church functionary, but even when such understanding has been provided with scrupulous detail the full story of faith and skepticism has not been told.

CHAPTER FIVE

CONCLUSION

In the present essay some of the implications of Kierkegaard's statement "Faith is a happy passion" have been explored in terms of a dispositional analysis. By this use of a technique from contemporary analytic philosophy certain features of the Christian faith, as represented by Kierkegaard, are brought into the context of current philosophical discussion.

The effect of analyzing the Christian faith in terms of the dispositions involved is primarily to expose the crucial position of the religious practices and tendencies within which the content of faith has its life--to stress the "how," as Kierkegaard would say, which fits the "what." This result, in turn, casts light on some questions about the nature of religious knowledge and about the possibility of communication between skeptics and believers.

A. Dispositional Analysis

Analytic Philosophy: The expression "dispositional analysis" is set down here with some hesitation. That such an analysis of mental concepts has limitations has been shown from the writings of Ryle and Peters which employ this approach.[1] The treatment of human emotions either in terms of regularities or of breakdowns looks very much like a vestige of the machinelike mind which Descartes postulated.

Even when the analogies from machines and from physical processes are not brought into play, and dispositions are handled as distinctively human phenomena, the application of the disposition concept to such questions as the relationship of faith and knowledge is not an obvious and easy one. Where knowledge and faith are treated as disposition concepts there is a temptation to reduce religious knowledge to a "knack" or to an easily acquired skill.[2]

---

[1] See *supra*, Chapter One, Sections C, D, and E, pp. 13-38.

[2] See *supra*, Chapter Three, pp. 76-91.

Despite the dangers in the use of the "dispositional analysis" formula, however, the disposition concept, properly applied, can be of value in helping us to avoid certain persistent puzzles which arise in the philosophy of religion with respect to mental concepts. Some of the major problems with such concepts as knowledge and emotion, for example, come up when, under the influence of the reason/passion distinction, mental concepts are enlisted in a supposed warfare between the cognitive and emotive faculties, with knowledge marching under the banner of truth, light, and order, and emotion drafted to fight for error, darkness, and chaos. Perhaps, as with so many philosophical problems, there is no solution which can be proposed which will finally negotiate the dispute. Yet if both knowledge and emotion are analyzed in terms of dispositions, it at least becomes extremely difficult to maintain in concrete cases the sharp division between the cognitive and emotive faculties which the faculty theory requires.[3]

Kierkegaard: When the concept of disposition is used in discussing Kierkegaard's treatment of the "how" of the Christian faith, a number of other qualifications are appropriate in addition to those cited above:

(1) The impression which is sometimes given[4] that dispositions are primarily patterns of publicly observable behavior meets with a powerful corrective from Kierkegaard. Kierkegaard does not in the least minimize the importance of actions[5] nor does he on the other hand postulate inner processes in order to account for actions; but he nevertheless provides an account of human life which does full justice to the interiority of the individual.

(2) Far from reducing the "how" of Christianity to a "knack," Kierkegaard portrays faith as a task of such strenuousness that we wonder whether such dispositions may ever be

---

[3] Peters comes very close to a mild version of the cognitive-emotive division in his theory of the emotions which we have stated *supra*, pp. 27-30, but even this restatement of the division is implausible in certain concrete cases.

[4] Above all by Ryle; see *supra*, Chapter Two, pp. 58-59.

[5] As opposed to Popkin; see *supra*, Chapter Two, p. 59, footnote 55.

Dispositional Analysis 127

achieved at all.[6] Climacus is out to "up the price" of Christianity to the cost which anyone who is faithful will have to pay; and that cost is, under normal circumstances, obloquy, suffering, and likely death through martyrdom.

(3) Kierkegaard is emphatic on the utter distinctiveness of the set of dispositions which is involved in faith. So specific are they, in fact, that if the "how" is given, the "what" is also given. Only one "what" will fit the Christian "how." This is Kierkegaard's answer to the position which we have called above "monism," which as it appears in the philosophy of religion implies that only the "what" of Christianity is distinctive, or that neither the "what" nor the "how" is distinctive.[7]

(4) It follows that Kierkegaard's dispositional analysis of the "how" of the Christian life does not in any way diminish the importance of the "what." The effect is only to show the roots of the intelligibility of the "what" by pointing to its matching "how." Kierkegaard did not believe that the real problem of those who questioned Christianity in his day was with its content; the "what" of faith was for the most part taken for granted. His words have special point today when the objection is often raised that the difficulty which men have with Christianity is not with its truth but its intelligibility.

Kierkegaard and Theorizing About the Passions: While Kierkegaard's portrayal of faith in the Climacus writings is by no means exhausted by the approach we have followed, the choice of the "how" or the dispositional side of faith as the point from which to develop the exposition does illumine the topic in an important way, and represents, moreover, the emphasis of Climacus himself.

Is there any way in which Kierkegaard contributes through the *Fragments* and the *Postscript* to a general understanding of the possibility of a dispositional analysis of mental concepts? Perhaps here, too, there is a contribution to be made. Kierkegaard's pseudonymous works are never easy, and the Climacean corpus is certainly not the simplest of these. Nevertheless,

---

[6] See *supra*, pp. 51, 53, 88-90.

[7] See *supra*, especially pp. 78, 87, 98-108. For Kierkegaard's distinctiveness cf. *supra*, pp. 89-91.

what Climacus tells us about the "how" of the passion of faith has an unmatched integrity, sensitivity, and richness of detail, which could make it a paradigm for dispositional analyses of other concepts.

On the other hand, it would be a mistake to look within the Climacus writings for a general theory of dispositions or of passions. Kierkegaard's practice typically is to avoid assuming a unitary sense for a broad concept such as passion, which functions in so many areas and so many ways, and to rely instead upon analogies to certain clear cases of the concept--in the case of passion, to love.[8] By this procedure he is able to map out some aspects of the concept of faith using some coordinates from the concept of love, and thus to clarify the concept of faith for certain purposes for certain people. His analogies are very helpful ones, and it is hard to see why--with the *Dozenten*, he would say--we need to "go beyond"[9] them to produce an overall theory.

Indeed, the quest for such a theory is surely an impossible one, if it is taken to require that the theory be perfectly general, accounting for all the complexities of the concept and allowing for all the exceptions. Perhaps Descartes or Spinoza envisioned something of this kind. But no theory can be altogether general in this sense. Otherwise the resulting "theory" would be nothing less than a mirror image of ordinary language itself, and as such it would cease to be a theory. It would be at once so intricate that it could never be set down, and so obvious that no one would be interested in hearing about it because all would know it already. The knowledge the "theory" would give would be of a "Socratic"[10] sort, since one would only need to be reminded to know that it had been in one's possession all the time. The search for an all-purpose clarification is a tantalizing one, but there is no more reason to suppose that we could find such

---

[8] See *supra*, pp. 62-63.

[9] For this Climacean phrase, see *Fragments*, p. 34. Cf. p. 139.

[10] *Fragments*, Chapter One.

a solution than that, to follow the previous analogy, we could produce an all-purpose map.[11]

B. Kierkegaard and Wittgenstein

Wittgenstein and Analytic Philosophy: Although the preceding parallel drawn between the analyses of mental concepts by some analytic philosophers and those by Kierkegaard points to genuine affinities between them, the differences exposed are great, even though they are not very easy to pin down. The most important among these differences is in the conception of philosophy itself. Through his portrait of the passion of faith Kierkegaard is not simply correcting a theory, but also correcting a method of theorizing. Kierkegaard's own mode of philosophizing is indirect and allusive, full of anecdotes and of dazzling changes of literary style. He has a deep-seated distrust of large-scale theories,[12] however ordinary they may appear and however diffidently they may be trotted out. Consequently he not only frequently begins with concrete examples, but he also keeps very close to particular problems and the particular people (for example his pseudonymous authors) for whom they are problems.

In this respect Kierkegaard is much closer to Wittgenstein[13] than to any of the other philosophers who are in the analytic tradition. And in fact the affinities between Kierkegaard and analytic philosophy which we have charted could very well have been drawn between Kierkegaard and Wittgenstein. The notions of "knowing how" and of dispositional analysis are developed brilliantly by Wittgenstein, starting from such utterances as the following:

---

[11]Such a map would in fact be on the grand scale of that mentioned by the German Professor in Lewis Carroll's *Sylvia and Bruno Concluded*, Chapter 11; "Mein Herr" tells how the cartographers of his country experimented with larger and larger maps until they finally made one with a scale of a mile to a mile! "It has never been spread out, yet," he says. "The farmers objected: they said it would cover the whole country, and shut out the sunlight! So now we use the country itself, as its own map, and I assure you it does nearly as well." (*Complete Works of Lewis Carroll* [New York, n.d.], p. 617.)

[12]Including his own; see *supra*, p. 45.

[13]See especially *supra*, pp. 65, 93, and footnote 50, pp. 110-11.

> The grammar of the word "knows" is evidently closely
> related to that of "can," "is able to." But also
> closely related to that of "understands." ('Mastery'
> of a technique,)[14]

The reason we have used other philosophers than Wittgenstein in order to make the parallel between Kierkegaard and analytic philosophy is that Wittgenstein writes in such an indirect style that it is not easy to fix his position as briefly as it is with a man like Ryle.

Passions and "Language Games": The relationship between Kierkegaard and Wittgenstein suggests a way in which their different presentations of the concept of understanding can be made to supplement each other.

An objection which is frequently raised to the program of interpreting human actions on the model of games is that, on such a basis, understanding the actions would be simply a matter of knowing what were the rules; in which case we would have to say that we could "understand" many pieces of utter nonsense, just as long as we could state the rules. What this criticism overlooks is that in order to "understand" an action in any important sense one needs not only to be able to cite the rules for that action, but also to be able to appreciate the point of what is done.

Nevertheless, the plausibility of the criticism points to a weakness in the metaphor of "language games." "If you know the rules, you know the game; all you need to do is follow instructions"--this is the immediate reaction of a typical person to the notion of understanding through language games. Such a person is forgetting an aspect of games which he would never forget about his other activities in life: that to understand an activity means not merely to be able to cite the rules given in the instruction manual, but also to see the point of behaving in that way.

It is at this place that calling faith a passion becomes helpful. Within the philosophical tradition describing faith as a passion is a very farfetched metaphor. But precisely for this reason it may be good to introduce the notion that faith is a passion into the philosophical discussion of the logic of faith;

---

[14]*Philosophical Investigations* (Oxford, 1958), I #150.

for the metaphor may serve to supplement our diet of examples,[15] and thus serve as a corrective to the sole reliance on the metaphor of games. The person who sees faith as a game may know all the rules but fail to see the point of acting that way; whereas the one who is taken up with the passion of faith will find it needless to ask about the point of the activity, but he may have difficulty stating any rules, and might indeed find the rules an intrusion.

Kierkegaard: Understanding Faith in Deer Park: In the passage which we cited in an earlier chapter, Climacus tells the story of the "spy" who goes about in Deer Park in Copenhagen in order to discover whether the parishioners understood the sermon last Sunday on the text: "A man can do nothing of himself, but with God he can do everything."[16] The "spy" discovers that the parishioners, who thought on Sunday that they understood the text perfectly well, do not have the "how" which is the condition for understanding what the parson has said.

What sort of understanding of faith is it which the parishioners lack? Through his *analogia amoris* Climacus suggests the answer: they do not know "how" the text could be lived; and even if they could recite the rules for the appropriate behavior (through having heard stories of suffering and martyrdom) they do not see the point of acting in that way. As a result these parishioners are neither believers nor skeptics, but men without a certain human passion. For faith is a passion, and the only men who understand it are those who understand it passionately-- the happy and the unhappy lovers, the passionate believer and the passionate skeptic.

Kierkegaard's concept of passionate faith is thus in the end not a new theory of faith, a new "what" to replace the old, but a call for integrity in the Christian "how." There is a temptation in theology toward a kind of "intellectualist legend" that the way in which to make the Christian faith secure is to formalize the "how" within a "what." In this tradition of theology there are many volumes on sanctification, regeneration, and all the other inner processes of a Christian. Kierkegaard's

---

[15]*Ibid.*, I #593.

[16]See *supra*, pp. 45-47.

point is a simple one: however far one goes, however many volumes are written, one must ultimately come to an unformalized "how."[17] Kierkegaard insists that we reckon not only with religious belief but with the believer, not only with articles of faith but with faithfulness. Sooner or later the analysis of faith must arrive at the "how," the passion of faith.

---

[17]"There are many, many envelopes--but there must be a point somewhere or other where we are brought up short, having at last met subjectivity." (X^2 A 301, quoted in Fabro, "Faith and Reason in Kierkegaard's Dialectic," p. 161.) Cf. *supra*, Chapter Three, p. 74, footnote 25.

BIBLIOGRAPHY

Abelson, Raziel. "Knowledge and Belief," *Journal of Philosophy*, LXV (November 21, 1968), 733-37.

Adams, E. M. "On Knowing That," *Philosophical Quarterly*, VIII (October, 1958), 300-06.

Allen, Diogenes. "Motives, Rationales, and Religious Beliefs," *American Philosophical Quarterly*, III (April, 1966), 111-27.

Alexander, Peter. "The Difficulties Which the Scientist Experiences in Accepting Theological Statements," *Christian Scholar*, XXXVIII (September, 1955), 206-18.

_____. *Sensationalism and Scientific Explanation*. "Studies in Philosophical Psychology." London: Routledge and Kegan Paul, 1963.

Allison, Henry E. "Christianity and Nonsense," *Review of Metaphysics*, XX (March, 1967), 432-60.

Alston, William P. "Expressing," in *Philosophy in America*. Edited by Max Black. Ithaca, New York: Cornell University Press, 1965, 15-34.

_____. "Feelings," *Philosophical Review*, LXXVIII (January, 1969), 3-34.

Ammerman, Robert. "A Note on 'Knowing That'," *Analysis*, XVII (December, 1956), 30-32.

Anscombe, G. E. M. *Intention*. Oxford: Basil Blackwell, 1958.

Ayer, Alfred Jules. *Language, Truth and Logic*. Second Edition. New York: Dover Publications, 1946.

Bambrough, Renford. "Universals and Family Resemblances," *Proceedings of the Aristotelian Society*, LXI (1960-61), 207-22.

Barth, Karl. "A Thank You and a Bow: Kierkegaard's Reveille," translated from the German by H. Martin Rumscheidt, *Canadian Journal of Theology*, XI (January, 1965), 3-7.

_____. "Notes and Comments: Kierkegaard and the Theologians," translated from the German by H. Martin Rumscheidt, *Canadian Journal of Theology*, XIII (January, 1967), 64-65.

Bedford, Errol. "Emotions," in *The Philosophy of Mind*. Edited by V. C. Chappell. Englewood Cliffs, N. J.: Prentice-Hall, 1962, 110-26.

Bell, D. R. "The Idea of a Social Science," *Proceedings of the Aristotelian Society, Supplementary Volume*, XLI (1967), 115-31.

Benson, John. "Emotion and Expression," *Philosophical Review*, LXXVI (July, 1967), 335-57.

Bird, G. N. "Mr. Hampshire on Dispositions," *Analysis*, XIV (March, 1954), 100-02.

Black, Max. "Metaphor," in *Models and Metaphors*. Ithaca, New York: Cornell University Press, 1962, 25-47.

Braithwaite, R. B. "Half-Belief," *Proceedings of the Aristotelian Society, Supplementary Volume*, XXXIII (1964), 163-74.

_____. "An Empiricist's View of the Nature of Religious Belief," in *Christian Ethics and Contemporary Philosophy*. Edited by Ian T. Ramsey. London: SCM Press, 1966, 53-73. (This article is a reprint of the Eddington Memorial Lecture delivered at Oxford in 1955 and later published by the Cambridge University Press.)

_____. "Discussion" (following his lecture "An Empiricist's View of the Nature of Religious Belief"), in *Christian Ethics and Contemporary Philosophy*. Edited by Ian T. Ramsey. London: SCM Press, 1966, 88-94.

Cameron, J. M. *The Night Battle: Essays*. London: Burns and Oates, 1962.

Camus, Albert. *The Rebel: An Essay on Man in Revolt*. New York: Vintage Books, 1956.

Carroll, Lewis [Charles L. Dodgson]. *Complete Works*. New York: The Modern Library, n.d.

Cavell, Stanley. "Existentialism and Analytical Philosophy," *Daedalus* (Summer, 1964), 946-74.

Chappell, V. C. (ed.). *The Philosophy of Mind*. Englewood Cliffs, N. J.: Prentice-Hall, 1962.

Christian, William A. *Meaning and Truth in Religion*. Princeton, N. J.: Princeton University Press, 1964.

Clarke, Norris, S. J. "It Is Compatible!" in *Faith and the Philosophers*. Edited by John Hick. London: Macmillan, 1964, 134-47.

_____. "A Further Critique of MacIntyre's Thesis," in *Faith and the Philosophers*. Edited by John Hick. London: Macmillan, 1964, 147-50.

Climacus, Johannes (pseud.). See Kierkegaard, Søren.

Coburn, Robert C. "A Neglected Use of Theological Language," *Mind*, LXXII (July, 1963), 369-85.

Descartes, René. "The Passions of the Soul," in *The Philosophical Works of Descartes*. Translated by Elizabeth S. Haldane and G. R. T. Ross. 2 Volumes. New York: Dover Publications, 1955, I, 332-427.

Bibliography

Diem, Hermann. *Kierkegaard's Dialectic of Existence*. Translated by Harold Knight. Edinburgh: Oliver and Boyd, 1959.

──────. *Dogmatics*. Translated by Harold Knight. Edinburgh: Oliver and Boyd, 1959.

──────. "Kierkegaard's Bequest to Theology," translated by Thora Moulton, in *A Kierkegaard Critique: An International Selection of Essays Interpreting Kierkegaard*. Edited by Howard A. Johnson and Niels Thulstrup. New York: Harper and Brothers, 1962, 244-65.

Eller, Vernard. *Kierkegaard and Radical Discipleship: A New Perspective*. Princeton, N.J.: Princeton University Press, 1968.

──────. "Fact, Faith, and Foolishness: Kierkegaard and the New Quest," *The Journal of Religion*, XLVIII (January, 1968), 54-68.

Ewing, A. C. "The Justification of Emotions," *Proceedings of the Aristotelian Society, Supplementary Volume*, XXXI (1957), 59-74.

Fabro, Cornelio, C. P. S. "Faith and Reason in Kierkegaard's Dialectic," in *A Kierkegaard Critique: An International Selection of Essays Interpreting Kierkegaard*. Edited by Howard A. Johnson and Niels Thulstrup. New York: Harper and Brothers, 1962, 156-206.

Flew, Antony. *God and Philosophy*. New York: Harcourt, Brace and World, 1966.

Fodor, Jerry A. "The Appeal to Tacit Knowledge in Psychological Explanation," *Journal of Philosophy*, LXV (October 24, 1968), 627-40.

Frankena, William K. "Some Aspects of Language," in *Language, Thought, and Culture*. Edited by Paul Henle. Ann Arbor, Michigan: University of Michigan Press, 1965, 121-45.

Gallie, W. B. "Essentially Contested Concepts," *Proceedings of the Aristotelian Society*, LVI (1955-56), 167-98. Reprinted in: *The Importance of Language*. Edited by Max Black. Englewood Cliffs, N. J.: Prentice-Hall, 1962, 121-46.

──────. *Philosophy and the Historical Understanding*. Second Edition. New York: Schocken Books, 1968.

Gardiner, H. N., Metcalfe, R. C., and Beebe-Center, J. G. *Feelings and Emotions: A History of Theories*. New York: American Book Company, 1937.

Garelick, Herbert M. "The Irrationality and Supra-rationality of Kierkegaard's Paradox," *Southern Journal of Philosophy*, II (Summer, 1964), 75-86.

──────. *The Anti-Christianity of Kierkegaard: A Study of Concluding Unscientific Postscript*. The Hague: Martinus Nijhoff, 1965.

Geach, Peter. "Nominalism," *Sophia*, III (July, 1964), 3-14.

Gellner, Ernest. "Knowing How and Validity," *Analysis*, XII (December, 1951), 25-35.

Götlind, Erik. *Three Theories of Emotion: Some Views on Philosophical Method.* Lund: C. W. K. Gleerup, 1958.

Gosling, J. C. "Emotion and Object," *Philosophical Review*, LXXIV (October, 1965), 486-503.

Hamlyn, D. W. "Behavior," *Philosophy*, XXVIII (1953), 132-45. Reprinted in: *The Philosophy of Mind.* Edited by V. C. Chappell. Englewood Cliffs, N. J.: Prentice-Hall, 1962, 60-73.

Hampshire, Stuart. "Review of Gilbert Ryle, *The Concept of Mind*," *Mind*, LIX (April, 1950), 237-55.

_____. "Dispositions," *Analysis*, XIV (October, 1953), 5-11.

_____. *Thought and Action.* London: Chatto and Windus, 1959.

_____. "Disposition and Memory." The Ernest Jones Lecture delivered before the British Psycho-Analytical Association on 15 June 1960. (Typewritten manuscript.)

_____. *Feeling and Expression.* An Inaugural Lecture delivered at University College London, 25 October 1960. London: Published for the College by H. K. Lewis, 1961.

_____. *Spinoza.* Revised Edition. London: Penguin Books, 1962.

Hartland-Swann, John. "The Logical Status of 'Knowing That'," *Analysis*, XVI (March, 1956), 111-15.

_____. "'Knowing That'--A Reply to Mr. Ammerman," *Analysis*, XVII (January, 1957), 69-71.

_____. "The Logic of 'Knowing Jones'," *Philosophical Studies*, VIII (January-February, 1957), 1-7.

Henze, Donald F. "Language-Games and the Ontological Argument," *Religious Studies*, IV (October, 1968), 147-52.

Hick, John. *Philosophy of Religion.* Second Edition. Englewood Cliffs, N. J.: Prentice-Hall, 1963.

_____. "Sceptics and Believers," in *Faith and the Philosophers.* Edited by John Hick. London: Macmillan, 1964, 235-50.

_____. *Faith and Knowledge.* Second Edition. Ithaca, New York: Cornell University Press, 1966.

High, Dallas M. *Language, Persons, and Belief: Studies in Wittgenstein's Philosophical Investigations and Religious Uses of Language.* New York: Oxford University Press, 1967.

Hofstadter, Albert. "Professor Ryle's Category-Mistake," *Journal of Philosophy*, XLVIII (April 26, 1951), 257-70.

Bibliography

Holland, R. F. "Morality and the Two Worlds Concept," *Proceedings of the Aristotelian Society*, LVI (1955-56), 45-62. Reprinted in: *Christian Ethics and Contemporary Philosophy*. Edited by Ian T. Ramsey. London: SCM Press, 1966, 299-313.

_____. "Religious Discourse and Theological Discourse," *Australasian Journal of Philosophy*, XXXIV (December, 1956), 147-63.

_____. "Modern Philosophers Consider Religion: A Reply," *Australasian Journal of Philosophy*, XXXVI (December, 1958), 208-09.

_____. "The Miraculous," in *Religion and Understanding*. Edited by D. Z. Phillips. Oxford: Basil Blackwell, 1967, 155-70.

Holmer, Paul L. "Kierkegaard and Religious Propositions," *Journal of Religion*, XXXV (July, 1955), 135-45.

_____. "On Understanding Kierkegaard," in *A Kierkegaard Critique: An International Selection of Essays Interpreting Kierkegaard*. Edited by Howard A. Johnson and Niels Thulstrup. New York: Harper and Brothers, 1962, 40-53.

_____. "Kierkegaard as a Critic," *Religion on Campus*, I (Spring, 1965), 4-7, 10.

_____. "Wittgenstein and Theology," *Reflection*, LXV (May, 1968), 1-4.

Hudson, W. Donald. "An Attempt to Defend Theism," *Philosophy*, XXXIX (January, 1964), 18-28.

_____. *Ludwig Wittgenstein: The Bearing of His Philosophy Upon Religious Belief*. Richmond, Virginia: John Knox Press, 1968.

_____. "Discussion: On Two Points Against Wittgensteinian Fideism," *Philosophy*, XLIII (July, 1968), 269-73.

Hume, David. *A Treatise of Human Nature*. Edited by L. A. Selby-Bigge. Oxford: Clarendon Press, 1958.

Hunter, J. F. M. "'Forms of Life' in Wittgenstein's *Philosophical Investigations*," *American Philosophical Quarterly*, V (October, 1968), 233-43.

James, William. *The Principles of Psychology*. Volume Two. New York: Dover Publications, 1950.

Kenny, Anthony. *Action, Emotion and Will*. "Studies in Philosophical Psychology." London: Routledge and Kegan Paul, 1963.

Kierkegaard, Søren. *Samlede Vaerker*. 14 Volumes. Edited by A. B. Drachmann, J. L. Heiberg and H. O. Lange. Kjøbenhavn: Gyldendalske Boghandels Forlag (F. Hegel og Søn), 1901-1906.

Kierkegaard, Søren. *Papirer*. 20 Volumes. Edited by P. A. Heiberg and V. Kuhr. Kjøbenhavn: Gyldendalske Boghandel, Nordisk Forlag, 1909-1929.

_____. *The Journals of Søren Kierkegaard*. Unabridged Edition. A Selection Edited and Translated by Alexander Dru. London: Oxford University Press, 1938.

_____. *Christian Discourses and the Lilies of the Field and the Birds of the Air and Three Discourses at the Communion on Fridays*. Translated with an Introduction by Walter Lowrie. London: Oxford University Press, 1940.

_____ [Johannes Climacus, pseud.]. *Concluding Unscientific Postscript to the Philosophical Fragments*. Translated by David F. Swenson and Walter Lowrie. Princeton, N. J.: Princeton University Press, 1941.

_____. *Training in Christianity and the Edifying Discourse Which "Accompanied" It*. Translated with an Introduction and Notes by Walter Lowrie. London: Oxford University Press, 1941.

_____. *Either/Or: A Fragment of Life*. 2 Volumes. Translated by David F. Swenson and Lillian Marvin Swenson. Princeton, N. J.: Princeton University Press, 1944.

_____. *Fear and Trembling and The Sickness Unto Death*. Translated with Introductions and Notes by Walter Lowrie. Garden City, New York: Doubleday, 1955.

_____. *Attack Upon "Christendom" 1854-1855*. Translated, with an Introduction by Walter Lowrie. Boston: Beacon Press, 1956.

_____. *The Concept of Dread*. Translated with Introduction and Notes by Walter Lowrie. Second Edition. Princeton, N. J.: Princeton University Press, 1957.

_____ [Johannes Climacus, pseud.]. *Johannes Climacus or, De Omnibus Dubitandum est and a Sermon*. Translated, with an Assessment, by T. H. Croxall. Stanford, California: Stanford University Press, 1958.

_____ [Johannes Climacus, pseud.]. *Philosophical Fragments or A Fragment of Philosophy*. Translated by David F. Swenson and Howard V. Hong. Introduction and Commentary by Niels Thulstrup. Princeton, N. J.: Princeton University Press, 1962.

_____. *Works of Love: Some Christian Reflections in the Form of Discourses*. Translated by Howard and Edna Hong. New York: Harper and Row, 1962.

_____. *The Present Age*. Translated by Alexander Dru. New York: Harper and Row, 1962.

_____. *The Prayers of Kierkegaard*. Edited and with a New Interpretation of His Life and Thought by Perry D. LeFevre. Chicago: University of Chicago Press, 1963.

Bibliography

Kierkegaard, Søren. *The Last Years: Journals 1853-1855*. Edited and Translated by Ronald Gregor Smith. London: Collins, 1965.

_____. *The Concept of Irony: With Constant Reference to Socrates*. Translated with an Introduction and Notes by Lee M. Capel. New York: Harper and Row, 1965.

_____. *On Authority and Revelation: The Book on Adler, or a Cycle of Ethico-Religious Essays*. Translated, with an Introduction and Notes, by Walter Lowrie. New York: Harper and Row, 1966.

_____. *Journals and Papers*. Volume 1, A-E. Edited and Translated by Howard V. Hong and Edna H. Hong. Assisted by Gregor Malantschuk. Bloomington, Indiana: Indiana University Press, 1967.

_____. *Stages on Life's Way*. Translated by Walter Lowrie. New York: Schocken Books, 1967.

King, Hugh R. "Professor Ryle and *The Concept of Mind*," *Journal of Philosophy*, XLVIII (April 26, 1951), 280-96.

Koller, Alice Ruth. "The Concept of Emotion: A Study of the Analyses of James, Russell, and Ryle." Unpublished Doctoral Dissertation, Radcliffe College, Cambridge, Massachusetts; April, 1960. (Typewritten manuscript.)

Lindström, Valter. "The Problem of Objectivity and Subjectivity in Kierkegaard," translated by Niels Erik Enkvist, in *A Kierkegaard Critique: An International Selection of Essays Interpreting Kierkegaard*. Edited by Howard A. Johnson and Niels Thulstrup. New York: Harper and Brothers, 1962, 228-43.

Lönning, Per. *The Dilemma of Contemporary Theology: Prefigured in Luther, Pascal, Kierkegaard, Nietzsche*. Oslo: Universitetsforlaget, 1962.

Löwith, Karl. *From Hegel to Nietzsche: The Revolution in Nineteenth-Century Thought*. Translated by David E. Green. Garden City, New York: Doubleday, 1967.

Louch, A. R. "The Very Idea of a Social Science," *Inquiry*, VI (Winter, 1963), 273-86.

_____. *Explanation and Human Action*. Oxford: Basil Blackwell, 1966.

Lucas, J. R. "The Soul," in *Faith and Logic: Oxford Essays in Philosophical Theology*. Edited by Basil Mitchell. London: George Allen and Unwin, 1957, 132-48.

_____. "On Not Worshipping Facts," *Philosophical Quarterly*, VIII (April, 1958), 144-56.

_____. "The Philosophy of the Reasonable Man," *Philosophical Quarterly*, XIII (April, 1963), 97-106.

Lucas, J. R. "Not 'Therefore' But 'But'," *Philosophical Quarterly*, XVI (October, 1966), 289-307.

MacDonald, Margaret. "Professor Ryle on The Concept of Mind," *Philosophical Review*, LX (January, 1951), 80-90.

Mace, C. A. "Emotions and the Category of Passivity," *Proceedings of the Aristotelian Society*, LXII (1961-62), 135-42.

MacIntyre, Alasdair C. "The Logical Status of Religious Belief," in *Metaphysical Beliefs: Three Essays*. London: SCM Press, 1957, 169-211.

_____. *The Unconscious: A Conceptual Analysis*. "Studies in Philosophical Psychology." London: Routledge and Kegan Paul, 1958.

_____. *Difficulties in Christian Belief*. London: SCM Press, 1959.

_____. "A Mistake About Causality in Social Science," in *Philosophy, Politics, and Society*. Second Series. Edited by Peter Laslett and W. G. Runciman. Oxford: Basil Blackwell, 1962, 48-70.

_____. "God and the Theologians," *Encounter*, XXI (September, 1963), 3-10.

_____. "Freudian and Christian Dogmas as Equally Unverifiable," in *Faith and the Philosophers*. Edited by John Hick. London: Macmillan, 1964, 110-11.

_____. "Is Understanding Religion Compatible with Believing?" in *Faith and the Philosophers*. Edited by John Hick. London: Macmillan, 1964, 115-33.

_____. "The Antecedents of Action," in *British Analytical Philosophy*. Edited by Bernard Williams and Alan Montefiore. London: Routledge and Kegan Paul, 1966, 205-25.

_____. *Secularization and Moral Change*. London: Oxford University Press, 1967.

_____. "The Idea of a Social Science," *Proceedings of the Aristotelian Society, Supplementary Volume*, XLI (1967), 95-114.

MacKinnon, D. M. "Discussion" (following Braithwaite's lecture "An Empiricist's View of the Nature of Religious Belief"), in *Christian Ethics and Contemporary Philosophy*. Edited by Ian T. Ramsey. London: SCM Press, 1966, 77-84.

MacMurray, John. *Reason and Emotion*. Second Edition. London: Faber and Faber, 1962.

McKinnon, Alastair. "'Religious Language' and the Assumptions of Belief," *Christian Scholar*, XLIX (Spring, 1966), 50-59.

_____. "Kierkegaard: 'Paradox' and Irrationalism," *Journal of Existentialism*, XXVII (Spring, 1967), 401-16.

McKinnon, Alastair. "Barth's Relation to Kierkegaard: Some Further Light," *Canadian Journal of Theology*, XIII (January, 1967), 31-41.

_____. "Kierkegaard's Pseudonyms: A New Hierarchy," *American Philosophical Quarterly*, VI (April, 1969), 116-26.

Malcolm, Norman. "Wittgenstein's *Philosophical Investigations*," *Philosophical Review*, LXIII (1954), 530-59. Reprinted in *The Philosophy of Mind*. Edited by V. C. Chappell. Englewood Cliffs, N. J.: Prentice-Hall, 1962, 74-100.

_____. *Ludwig Wittgenstein: A Memoir*. London: Oxford University Press, 1958.

_____. "Anselm's Ontological Arguments," *Philosophical Review*, LXIX (January, 1960), 41-62. Reprinted in *Religion and Understanding*. Edited by D. Z. Phillips. Oxford: Basil Blackwell, 1967, 43-61.

_____. *Knowledge and Certainty: Essays and Lectures*. Englewood Cliffs, N. J.: Prentice-Hall, 1963.

_____. "Is It a Religious Belief That 'God Exists'?" in *Faith and the Philosophers*. Edited by John Hick. London: Macmillan, 1964, 103-10.

Marshall, G. D. "On Being Affected," *Mind*, LXXVII (April, 1968), 243-59.

Martin, C. B. *Religious Belief*. Ithaca, New York: Cornell University Press, 1959.

[Martin], Jane Roland. "On the Reduction of 'Knowing That' to 'Knowing How'," *Philosophical Review*, LXVII (1959), 379-88. Revised and Reprinted in *Language and Concepts in Education*. Edited by B. Othanel Smith and Robert H. Ennis. Chicago: Rand McNally, 1961, 59-71.

Matthews, Gareth B. "Theology and Natural Theology," *Journal of Philosophy*, LXI (January 30, 1964), 99-108.

Mavrodes, George I. "God and Verification," *Canadian Journal of Theology*, X (1964), 187-91.

Melden, A. I. "Action," in *Essays in Philosophical Psychology*. Edited by Donald F. Gustafson. Garden City, New York: Doubleday, 1964, 58-76.

Mellor, W. W. "Knowing, Believing and Behaving," *Mind*, LXXVI (July, 1967), 327-45.

Michalson, Carl. "Kierkegaard's Theology of Faith," *Religion in Life*, XXXII (Spring, 1963), 225-37.

Mitchell, Basil. "The Justification of Religious Belief," *Philosophical Quarterly*, XI (July, 1961), 213-26. Reprinted in *New Essays on Religious Language*. Edited by Dallas M. High. New York: Oxford University Press, 1969, 178-97.

Miller, Dickinson S. "'Descartes' Myth' and Professor Ryle's Fallacy," *Journal of Philosophy*, XLVIII (April 26, 1951), 270-80.

Moore, George Edward. "Wittgenstein's Lectures in 1930-33," in *Philosophical Papers*. New York: Collier Books, 1962, 247-318.

Niebuhr, Richard R. "Dread and Joyfulness: The View of Man as Affectional Being," *Religion in Life*, XXXI (Spring, 1962), 443-64.

Nielsen, Kai. "Religion and the Modern Predicament," *Humanist*, XVIII (1958), 25-31.

_____. "Reason in the Social Sciences," *Phylon Quarterly*, XIX (Fall, 1958), 297-305.

_____. "Is God So Powerful That He Doesn't Even Have To Exist?" in *Religious Experience and Truth: A Symposium*. Edited by Sidney Hook. New York: New York University Press, 1961, 270-81.

_____. "Morality and God: Some Questions for Mr. MacIntyre," *Philosophical Quarterly*, XII (April, 1962), 129-37.

_____. "'Christian Positivism' and the Appeal to Religious Experience," *Journal of Religion*, XLII (October, 1962), 248-61.

_____. "On Speaking of God," *Theoria*, XXVIII, Part 2 (1962), 110-37.

_____. "Eschatological Verification," *Canadian Journal of Theology*, IX (1963), 271-81.

_____. "Can Faith Validate God-Talk?" in *New Theology No. 1*. Edited by Martin E. Marty and Dean G. Peerman. New York: Macmillan, 1964, 131-49.

_____. "A Sceptic's Reply," in *Faith and the Philosophers*. Edited by John Hick. London: Macmillan, 1964, 229-32.

_____. "God and the Good: Does Morality Need Religion?" *Theology Today*, XXI (April, 1964), 47-58.

_____. "Linguistic Philosophy and 'The Meaning of Life'," *Cross Currents*, XIV (Summer, 1964), 313-34.

_____. "God-Talk," *Sophia*, III (October, 1964), 15-19.

_____. "Religious Perplexity and Faith," *Crane Review*, VIII (Fall, 1965), 1-17.

_____. "God and Verification Again," *Canadian Journal of Philosophy*, XI (1965), 135-41.

_____. "On Fixing the Reference Range of 'God'," *Religious Studies*, II (October, 1966), 13-36.

Bibliography

Nielsen, Kai. "Linguistic Philosophy and Beliefs," *Journal of Existentialism*, VI (Summer, 1966), 421-37.

_____. "Wittgensteinian Fideism," *Philosophy*, XLII (July, 1967), 191-209.

_____. "On Believing That God Exists," *Southern Journal of Philosophy*, V (Fall, 1967), 167-72.

_____. "Wittgensteinian Fideism Again: A Reply to Hudson," *Philosophy*, XLIV (January, 1969), 63-65.

Pears, D. F. "Causes and Objects of Some Feelings and Psychological Reactions," in *Philosophy of Mind*. Edited by Stuart Hampshire. New York: Harper and Row, 1966, 143-69.

Penelhum, Terence. "The Logic of Pleasure," in *Essays in Philosophical Psychology*. Edited by Donald F. Gustafson. Garden City, New York: Doubleday, 1964, 227-47.

Perkins, Moreland. "Emotion and Feeling," *Philosophical Review*, LXXV (April, 1966), 139-60.

_____. "Emotion and the Concept of Behavior: A Disproof of Philosophical Behaviorism," *American Philosophical Quarterly*, III (October, 1966), 291-98.

Peters, R. S. *The Concept of Motivation*. "Studies in Philosophical Psychology." London: Routledge and Kegan Paul, 1958.

_____. "Emotions and the Category of Passivity," *Proceedings of the Aristotelian Society*, LXII (1961-62), 117-34.

_____. "Education as Initiation," in *Philosophical Analysis and Education*. Edited by Reginald D. Archambault. London: Routledge and Kegan Paul, 1965, 87-111.

Phillips, Dewi Z. "Philosophy, Theology, and the Reality of God," *Philosophical Quarterly*, XIII (October, 1963), 344-50.

_____. "Does It Pay To Be Good?" *Proceedings of the Aristotelian Society, Supplementary Volume*, LXV (1964-65), 45-60.

_____. *The Concept of Prayer*. London: Routledge and Kegan Paul, 1965.

_____. "On Morality's Having a Point," *Philosophy*, XL (October, 1965), 308-19.

_____. "The Christian Concept of Love," in *Christian Ethics and Contemporary Philosophy*. Edited by Ian T. Ramsey. London: SCM Press, 1966, 314-28.

_____. "Religion and Epistemology: Some Contemporary Confusions," *Australasian Journal of Philosophy*, XXXIV (December, 1966), 316-30.

Phillips, Dewi Z. "Faith, Scepticism and Religious Understanding," in *Religion and Understanding*. Edited by D. Z. Phillips. Oxford: Basil Blackwell, 1967, 63-79.

_____. "From World to God?" *Proceedings of the Aristotelian Society*, Supplementary Volume, XLI (1967), 133-52.

_____. "Subjectivity and Religious Truth in Kierkegaard," *Sophia*, VII (July, 1968), 3-13.

_____. "Wisdom's Gods," *Philosophical Quarterly*, XIX (January, 1969), 15-32.

Pitcher, George. *The Philosophy of Wittgenstein*. Englewood Cliffs, N. J.: Prentice-Hall, 1964.

_____. "Emotion," *Mind*, LXXIV (July, 1965), 326-46.

Place, U. T. "The Concept of Heed," in *Essays in Philosophical Psychology*. Edited by Donald F. Gustafson. Garden City, New York: Doubleday, 1964, 206-26.

Popkin, Richard H. "Hume and Kierkegaard," *Journal of Religion*, XXXI (October, 1951), 274-81.

_____. "Theological and Religious Scepticism," *Christian Scholar*, XXXIX (June, 1956), 150-58.

_____. "Kierkegaard and Scepticism," *Algemeen Nederlands Tijdschrift voor Wijsbegeerte en Psychologie*, LI (1958), 123-41.

Powell, Betty. *Knowledge of Actions*. London: George Allen and Unwin, 1967.

Price, H. H. "Faith and Belief," in *Faith and the Philosophers*. Edited by John Hick. London: Macmillan, 1964, 3-25.

_____. "Half-Belief," *Proceedings of the Aristotelian Society*, Supplementary Volume, XXXVIII (1964), 148-62.

_____. "Belief 'In' and Belief 'That'," *Religious Studies*, I (October, 1965), 5-27.

_____. "Belief and Will," in *Philosophy of Mind*. Edited by Stuart Hampshire. New York: Harper and Row, 1966, 91-116.

_____. "On Believing--A Reply to Professor R. W. Sleeper," *Religious Studies*, II (April, 1967), 243-45.

Ramsey, Ian T. *Models and Mystery*. London: Oxford University Press, 1964.

_____. "Discussion" (following Braithwaite's lecture "An Empiricist's View of the Nature of Religious Belief"), in *Christian Ethics and Contemporary Philosophy*. Edited by Ian T. Ramsey. London: SCM Press, 1966, 84-88.

_____ (ed.). *Christian Ethics and Contemporary Philosophy*. London: SCM Press, 1966.

Rhees, Rush. "Can There Be a Private Language?" *Proceedings of the Aristotelian Society, Supplementary Volume*, XXVIII (1954), 77-94. Reprinted in: *Philosophy and Ordinary Language*. Edited by Charles E. Caton. Urbana, Illinois: University of Illinois Press, 1963, 90-107.

_____. "Preface," to Ludwig Wittgenstein, *Blue and Brown Books*. Oxford: Basil Blackwell, 1958, v-xiv.

_____. "Wittgenstein's Builders," *Proceedings of the Aristotelian Society*, LX (1959-60), 171-86. Reprinted in: *Ludwig Wittgenstein: The Man and His Philosophy*. Edited by K. T. Fann. New York: Delta Book, 1967, 251-64.

_____. "Some Developments in Wittgenstein's View of Ethics," *Philosophical Review*, LXXIV (January, 1965), 17-26.

Rorty, Richard. "Pragmatism, Categories and Language," *Philosophical Review*, LXX (April, 1961), 197-223.

_____. "Metaphilosophical Difficulties of Linguistic Philosophy," in *The Linguistic Turn: Recent Essays in Philosophical Method*. Edited by Richard Rorty. Chicago: University of Chicago Press, 1967, 1-39.

Roupas, Graham. "Emotions," *Graduate Review of Philosophy* (University of Minnesota), V (Spring, 1963), 4-9.

Ryle, Gilbert. *Philosophical Arguments*. Oxford: Clarendon Press, 1945.

_____. "Knowing How and Knowing That," *Proceedings of the Aristotelian Society*, XLVI (1945-46), 1-16.

_____. *The Concept of Mind*. New York: Barnes and Noble, 1949.

_____. "Thinking and Language," *Proceedings of the Aristotelian Society, Supplementary Volume*, XXV (1951), 65-73.

_____. "Feelings," *Philosophical Quarterly*, I (April, 1951), 193-205.

_____. "Ordinary Language," *Philosophical Review*, LXII (1953), 167-86. Reprinted in: *Ordinary Language*. Edited by V. C. Chappell. Englewood Cliffs, N. J.: Prentice-Hall, 1964, 24-40.

_____. *Dilemmas: The Tarner Lectures 1953*. Cambridge: Cambridge University Press, 1960.

_____. *A Rational Animal*. London: Athlone Press, 1962.

_____. "Systematically Misleading Expressions," in *Logic and Language*. First and Second Series. Edited by Antony Flew. Garden City, New York: Doubleday, 1965, 14-40.

_____. "Categories," in *Logic and Language*. First and Second Series. Edited by Antony Flew. Garden City, New York: Doubleday, 1965, 281-98.

Ryle, Gilbert. "Teaching and Training," in *The Concept of Education*. Edited by R. S. Peters. London: Routledge and Kegan Paul, 1967, 105-19.

Scheffler, Israel. "On Ryle's Theory of Propositional Knowledge," *Journal of Philosophy*, LXV (November 21, 1968), 725-32.

Schmidt, Paul F. "Is There Religious Knowledge?" *Journal of Philosophy*, LV (June 19, 1958), 529-38.

_____. *Religious Knowledge*. Glencoe, Illinois: Free Press, 1961.

_____. "Knowing-How in Religion," *Religious Humanism*, II (Spring, 1968), 80-84.

Schofield, J. N. "Discussion" (following Braithwaite's lecture "An Empiricist's View of the Nature of Religious Belief"), in *Christian Ethics and Contemporary Philosophy*. Edited by Ian T. Ramsey. London: SCM Press, 1966, 74-77.

Sleeper, R. W. "On Believing," *Religious Studies*, II (October, 1966), 75-93.

Smart, J. J. C. "The Existence of God," in *New Essays in Philosophical Theology*. Edited by Antony Flew and Alasdair MacIntyre. London: SCM Press, 1955, 28-46.

Smart, Ninian. "Social Anthropology and the Philosophy of Religion," *Inquiry*, VI (1963), 287-99.

Spinoza, Benedict de. *Ethics*. Edited by James Gutmann. New York: Hafner Publishing Company, 1949.

Thalberg, Irving. "Emotion and Thought," in *Philosophy of Mind*. Edited by Stuart Hampshire. New York: Harper and Row, 1966, 201-25.

_____. "Verbs, Deeds and What Happens to Us," *Theoria*, XXXIII, Part 3 (1967), 259-77.

Thomas, J. Heywood. *Subjectivity and Paradox*. Oxford: Basil Blackwell, 1957.

Toulmin, Stephen Edelston. "A Defence of 'Synthetic Necessary Truth'," *Mind*, LVIII (April, 1949), 164-77.

_____. "Concept-Formation in Philosophy and Psychology," in *Dimensions of Mind: A Symposium*. Edited by Sidney Hook. New York: Collier Books, 1960, 191-203.

_____. *The Uses of Argument*. Cambridge: Cambridge University Press, 1964.

Waismann, Friedrich. "Notes on Talks with Wittgenstein," translated by Max Black, *Philosophical Review*, LXXIV (January, 1965), 12-16.

Waismann, Friedrich. "Language Strata," in *Logic and Language*. First and Second Series. Edited by Antony Flew. Garden City, New York: Doubleday, 1965, 226-47.

Warnock, Mary. "The Justification of Emotions," *Proceedings of the Aristotelian Society*, Supplementary Volume, XXXI (1957), 43-58.

Weitz, Morris. "Professor Ryle's 'Logical Behaviorism'," *Journal of Philosophy*, XLVIII (April 26, 1951), 297-301.

White, Alan R. "Mr. Hampshire and Prof. Ryle on Dispositions," *Analysis*, XIV (April, 1954), 111-14.

_____. "Thinking That and Knowing That," *Philosophical Quarterly*, XI (1961), 68-73.

_____. *Attention*. Oxford: Basil Blackwell, 1964.

_____. *The Philosophy of Mind*. New York: Random House, 1967.

Williams, B. A. O. "Pleasure and Belief," in *Philosophy of Mind*. Edited by Stuart Hampshire. New York: Harper and Row, 1966, 225-42.

Winch, Peter. *The Idea of a Social Science and Its Relation to Philosophy*. London: Routledge and Kegan Paul, 1958.

_____. "Nature and Convention," *Proceedings of the Aristotelian Society*, LX (1959-60), 231-52.

_____. "Mr. Louch's Idea of a Social Science," *Inquiry*, VII (Summer, 1964), 202-08.

_____. "Understanding a Primitive Society," *American Philosophical Quarterly*, I (October, 1964), 307-24. Reprinted in: *Religion and Understanding*. Edited by D. Z. Phillips. Oxford: Basil Blackwell, 1967, 9-42.

_____. "Can a Good Man Be Harmed?" *Proceedings of the Aristotelian Society*, LXVI (1965-66), 55-70.

Wisdom, John. "The Concept of Mind," *Proceedings of the Aristotelian Society*, L (1949-50), 189-204. Reprinted in: *The Philosophy of Mind*. Edited by V. C. Chappell. Englewood Cliffs, N. J.: Prentice-Hall, 1962, 49-59.

Wittgenstein, Ludwig. *Tractatus Logico-Philosophicus*. London: Routledge and Kegan Paul, 1922.

_____. *The Blue and Brown Books*. Oxford: Basil Blackwell, 1958.

_____. *Philosophical Investigations*. Translated by G. E. M. Anscombe. Oxford: Basil Blackwell, 1958.

_____. *Philosophische Bemerkungen*. Aus dem Nachlass herausgegeben von Rush Rhees. Oxford: Basil Blackwell, 1964.

Wittgenstein, Ludwig. *Remarks on the Foundations of Mathematics*. Edited by G. H. von Wright, Rush Rhees, and G. E. M. Anscombe. Translated by G. E. M. Anscombe. Oxford: Basil Blackwell, 1964.

_____. (Lecture on Ethics.) *Philosophical Review*. LXXIV (January, 1965), 3-12.

_____. *Lectures and Conversations on Aesthetics, Psychology and Religious Belief*. Compiled from Notes Taken by Yorick Smythies, Rush Rhees, and James Taylor. Edited by Cyril Barrett. Oxford: Basil Blackwell, 1966.

_____. *Letters From Ludwig Wittgenstein With a Memoir*. Edited by Paul Engelmann. Oxford: Basil Blackwell, 1967.

_____. *Zettel*. Edited by G. E. M. Anscombe and G. H. von Wright. Translated by G. E. M. Anscombe. Oxford: Basil Blackwell, 1967.

_____. "Bemerkungen Über Frazers *The Golden Bough*," *Synthese*, XVII (September, 1967), 233-53.

Ziff, Paul. "About Behaviorism," *Analysis*, XVIII (1957-58), 132-36. Reprinted in: *The Philosophy of Mind*. Edited by V. C. Chappell. Englewood Cliffs, N. J.: Prentice-Hall, 1962, 147-50.

Zuurdeeg, Willem F. "Some Aspects of Kierkegaard's Language Philosophy," in *Filosofia Moderna*, Volume XII of *Atti del XII Congresso Internazionale di Filosofia* (Venezia 12-18 Settembre, 1958). Firenze: Sansone Editore, 1961, 493-99.